D1329613

WITHDRAWAL

Number 101
Spring 2004

MARYLAND UNIVERSITY
ARGARET SCHOOL OF EDUCATION
MONROE C. GUTMAN LIBRARY

New Directions for Evaluation

Jean A. King
Editor-in-Chief

Robin Miller
Katherine Ryan
Nancy Zajano
Associate Editors

Co-Constructing a Contextually Responsive Evaluation Framework

The Talent Development Model of School Reform

Veronica G. Thomas
Floraline I. Stevens
Editors

Co-Constructing a Contextually Responsive Evaluation Framework:
The Talent Development Model of School Reform
Veronica G. Thomas, Floraline I. Stevens (eds.)
New Directions for Evaluation, no. 101
Jean A. King, Editor-in-Chief
Copyright ©2004 Wiley Periodicals, Inc., A Wiley company

Microfilm copies of issues and articles are available in 16mm and 35mm, as well as microfiche in 105mm, through University Microfilms Inc., 300 North Zeeb Road, Ann Arbor, Michigan 48106-1346.

New Directions for Evaluation is indexed in Contents Pages in Education, Higher Education Abstracts, and Sociological Abstracts.

NEW DIRECTIONS FOR EVALUATION (ISSN 1097-6736, electronic ISSN 1534-875X) is part of The Jossey-Bass Education Series and is published quarterly by Wiley Subscription Services, Inc., a Wiley company, at Jossey-Bass, 989 Market Street, San Francisco, California 94103-1741.

SUBSCRIPTIONS cost $80.00 for U.S./Canada/Mexico; $104 international. For institutions, agencies, and libraries, $175 U.S.; $215 Canada; $249 international. Prices subject to change.

EDITORIAL CORRESPONDENCE should be addressed to the Editor-in-Chief, Jean A. King, University of Minnesota, 330 Wulling Hall, 86 Pleasant Street SE, Minneapolis, MN 55455.

www.josseybass.com

May 6, 2004

Editorial Policy and Procedures

New Directions for Evaluation, a quarterly sourcebook, is an official publication of the American Evaluation Association. The journal publishes empirical, methodological, and theoretical works on all aspects of evaluation. A reflective approach to evaluation is an essential strand to be woven through every volume. The editors encourage volumes that have one of three foci: (1) craft volumes that present approaches, methods, or techniques that can be applied in evaluation practice, such as the use of templates, case studies, or survey research; (2) professional issue volumes that present issues of import for the field of evaluation, such as utilization of evaluation or locus of evaluation capacity; (3) societal issue volumes that draw out the implications of intellectual, social, or cultural developments for the field of evaluation, such as the women's movement, communitarianism, or multiculturalism. A wide range of substantive domains is appropriate for *New Directions for Evaluation;* however, the domains must be of interest to a large audience within the field of evaluation. We encourage a diversity of perspectives and experiences within each volume, as well as creative bridges between evaluation and other sectors of our collective lives.

The editors do not consider or publish unsolicited single manuscripts. Each issue of the journal is devoted to a single topic, with contributions solicited, organized, reviewed, and edited by a guest editor. Issues may take any of several forms, such as a series of related chapters, a debate, or a long article followed by brief critical commentaries. In all cases, the proposals must follow a specific format, which can be obtained from the editor-in-chief. These proposals are sent to members of the editorial board and to relevant substantive experts for peer review. The process may result in acceptance, a recommendation to revise and resubmit, or rejection. However, the editors are committed to working constructively with potential guest editors to help them develop acceptable proposals.

Jean A. King, Editor-in-Chief
University of Minnesota
330 Wulling Hall
86 Pleasant Street SE
Minneapolis, MN 55455
e-mail: kingx004@umn.edu

SERIES EDITOR'S NOTES

I did not decide as a child to become either a program evaluator or the editor of a respected evaluation journal, but somewhere along the way, I got lucky and ended up becoming both. My term as editor of *New Directions for Evaluation* began in January 2004, following the six-year tenure of Jennifer Greene and Gary Henry as coeditors-in-chief. They have made my job easy in an important way. The twenty-two volumes they edited continued the tradition of thoughtful excellence that has long characterized this journal. (I should note that they also accepted the proposals for Volumes 101 and 102, and Jennifer Greene has provided extensive editorial support for these volumes.) In my experience, practicing evaluators and students alike welcome each issue as a succinct review of an important or novel development in the field that they ought to know about. Topics are presented full spectrum: *NDE* includes both the good and the bad and provides formal (but constructive) critique, helping readers to examine multiple sides of issues with open eyes. Established names in the field appear next to newcomers, evaluation theorists alongside practitioners. This is a tradition I will work hard to continue.

In addition, I celebrate the *NDE* proposal process, which differs from that of journals accepting individual articles. Allowing guest editors to develop entire volumes encourages both flexibility and creativity. Anyone in our extended field can put together a proposal, involving whomever they believe are the best writers on that subject. The *NDE* peer review and editorial process provides detailed and often interactive feedback, and our strong editorial board sets high standards indeed.

Newcomers to any task bring new ideas and hopes. In a special associate editor role, Katherine Ryan has agreed to develop an *NDE* student editorial board, building on procedures other journals have used and adapting them to the special nature of this journal. I hope that within the year, students studying in a variety of venues will find formal and informal opportunities to learn about evaluation in general and editorial work specifically through participation in *New Directions for Evaluation* activities.

Our new editorial team, which includes Robin Miller and Nancy Zajano in addition to Katherine Ryan and myself, aspires to provide the evaluation community high-quality thinking about evaluation theory and practice, supported when possible by empirical data and the best of current practice. We look forward to your help and feedback.

Jean A. King
Editor-in-Chief

CONTENTS

EDITORS' NOTES

This volume presents an approach for evaluating urban school reform interventions: the Talent Development evaluation framework. This approach, deeply embedded in the work of the Howard University Center for Research on the Education of Students Placed At Risk (CRESPAR) and the Talent Development Model of School Reform, embraces five major themes: engaging stakeholders, co-construction, responsiveness, cultural and contextual relevance, and triangulation of perspectives.

The CRESPAR Talent Development (TD) evaluation approach is rooted in several traditions of evaluation that intentionally seek engagement with contexts of practice: responsive, participatory, empowerment, and culturally competent approaches to evaluation. The approach also takes up themes of inclusiveness and partnership advanced by the recent promotion of multiple methods in evaluation. With these themes, the TD evaluation approach is grounded in well-accepted evaluation concepts and principles. The approach seeks to be practical, useful, formative, and empowering for the individuals being served by TD evaluations and to give voice to persons whose perspectives are often ignored, minimized, or rejected in urban school settings.

Beyond such grounding and ambitions, the CRESPAR TD evaluation framework seeks to reposition evaluation in low-income urban contexts as accountable not only for producing accurate and relevant information on the program being evaluated, but also for enabling and contributing to the program's social betterment and social justice intentions. This repositioning is effected primarily by a collaborative, co-constructionist model for evaluation in which CRESPAR program developers, implementers, and evaluators, along with key program stakeholders, partner in envisioning, implementing, and evaluating programs that are responsive to and make cultural sense in the context at hand. CRESPAR TD evaluators are contextually and culturally engaged and are responsible for this engagement.

In Chapter One, Veronica G. Thomas introduces the Talent Development Model of School Reform and the overarching framework for evaluating its intervention efforts. The four subsequent chapters provide illustrative case examples of the TD evaluation framework in practice. Velma LaPoint and Henry L. Jackson discuss in Chapter Two how they evaluated the co-construction of a school-based family, school, and community partnership program for black students in a low-income urban high school setting. In Chapter Three, Jo-Anne L. Manswell Butty, Malva Daniel Reid, and Velma LaPoint illuminate the successes and challenges they encountered in evaluating an urban school-to-career intervention using a culturally responsive approach. Discussing their study of exemplary urban schools in Chapter Four, Donna Penn Towns and Zewelanji Serpell describe how triangulating methodologies allowed for stakeholder involvement and revealed contexts and findings that a narrower approach would have failed to illuminate. Constance M. Ellison presents in Chapter Five a paradigm for evaluating professional development interventions in a manner consistent with the major tenets of the TD evaluation framework. In total, these chapters illustrate meaningful and authentic strategies for evaluating interventions serving low-income urban populations. The volume concludes with two commentaries by scholars external to the Howard University CRESPAR. Floraline I. Stevens comments in Chapter Six on the coherence of the TD evaluation framework as evident in the case study examples presented here. Finally, in Chapter Seven, Laurence Parker examines the utility of critical race theory in the evaluation of educational reform efforts in general, and in regard to the epistemological and methodological perspectives put forth by the TD paradigm in particular.

Many of the problems encountered in urban school-based evaluations are evident in other types of evaluations, particularly those conducted in communities serving underserved populations. Therefore, it is our hope that the conceptual, methodological, and strategic issues discussed in this volume have utility for substantive areas beyond the field of education.

This volume would not have happened without the ongoing support, encouragement, and feedback of Jennifer C. Greene and Jean A. King. Their critical insights and reviews significantly contributed to the quality and depth of material presented in the chapters. We are indeed grateful for their seeing this project to fruition.

Veronica G. Thomas
Floraline I. Stevens
Editors

VERONICA G. THOMAS is coprincipal investigator of the Secondary School Project at the Center for Research on the Education of Students Placed At Risk and professor in the Department of Human Development and Psychoeducational Studies, Howard University, Washington, D.C. She is also principal investigator of the Howard University Evaluation Training Institute.

FLORALINE I. STEVENS is president of Stevens and Associates, an evaluation and research consultant firm in Pasadena, California.

1

The chapter introduces the conceptual underpinnings and overarching themes of the Talent Development evaluation framework and provides recommendations for minimizing problems in implementing evaluations in diverse urban settings.

Building a Contextually Responsive Evaluation Framework: Lessons from Working with Urban School Interventions

Veronica G. Thomas

The past two decades have witnessed a significant growth in the number of school improvement programs and in the accompanying efforts to evaluate such programs (Slavin and Fashola, 1998). Passage of the No Child Left Behind (NCLB) Act in 2002 has intensified the need for evaluations to assess and understand the quality and value of educational interventions. Well over a decade ago, Oakes (1986) argued that evaluation studies of reform efforts did not attach particular importance to the fact that schools fail to serve all students equally well. In large part, this assertion is still relevant in the current climate of educational reform and evaluation. Schools are often viewed as neutral institutions, and their reforms are presented as color and affluence blind (Waters, 1998). Traditional school reform efforts fail to address such issues as the unequal quality of school facilities, programs, curricula, counseling, expectations, and instruction (Oakes and Guiton, 1995). Clearly, the contexts (both micro and macro) of urban schools make the design, implementation, and evaluation of school-based interventions complex matters.

The work reported herein was supported by grant(s) from the Institute of Education Sciences (IES) (formerly the Office of Educational Research and Improvement), U.S. Department of Education. The findings and opinions expressed in this chapter do not necessarily reflect the position or policies of the Institute of Education Sciences or the U.S. Department of Education.

The recent school reform movement has focused on raising student achievement, responding to demands from the general public and policy-makers alike. Special attention has been given to reforming public education for students who are most often placed at risk for academic failure: low-income, minority students in urban public schools (Boykin, 2000; Delpit, 1995; Noguera, 1996; Williams, 1996). Some of the more popular reform models implemented in schools that serve low-income and minority students include the Coalition of Essential Schools (Sizer, 1984, 1992, 1996), School Development Program (Comer, 1980; Comer, Haynes, Joyner, and Ben-Avie, 1996), Accelerated Schools (Hopfenberg and Levin, 1993; Levin, 1987), and Success for All (Slavin, Madden, Dolan, and Wasik, 1996). More recently, the Talent Development (TD) Model of School Reform (Boykin, 2000) was designed by the Center for Research on the Education of Students Placed At Risk (CRESPAR) as an alternative approach to educational reform that squarely addresses some of the cultural and contextual issues ignored, missed, or minimized in other reform models.

CRESPAR and the Talent Development Model of School Reform

CRESPAR was funded in 1994 by the U.S. Department of Education as a collaborative between Howard University and Johns Hopkins University. The center's mission is to conduct research, development, and evaluation activities needed to transform schooling for children who have historically fared poorly in our nation's schools. CRESPAR has successfully formulated, evaluated, and disseminated a comprehensive model of school reform, as well as separate academic programs that supplement key components of the model, both domestically and abroad (Boykin and Slavin, 2000; Engelbrecht and Rashid, 2002; Jagers, 2001; Rashid, 2000). Furthermore, CRESPAR has vigorously engaged in a variety of basic and applied research studies, collaborative interventions, evaluations, and scale-up dissemination activities, all aimed at transforming schools, particularly for children who, for a variety of reasons, have been placed at risk for educational failure.

CRESPAR's work is guided by the TD model, which asserts that all students can learn to high standards when key stakeholders are committed to such a goal and hold themselves to high standards. Although there are different conceptions of the terms *talent* and *development,* in conceptualizing the TD Model, Boykin (2000) used the term *talent* to refer to high-level performance, skill, understanding, or knowledge that is predicated on an age-appropriate standard of excellence. As such, the TD assertion that "all students can learn" should be understood to mean that virtually all students can attain a talented standard of general academic proficiency in school. As Boykin further notes, the term *development* is constructed as conveying multiple processes of student change. It refers to cultivating, fostering, and bringing talent to fruition; promoting and enhancing student talent, taking it to ever higher levels; identifying and validating talent, actively seeking out its manifestations and discerning its existence even when it is presumed not to be there; and sustaining student talent and keeping it from fading, especially at critical student development junctures. In addition, it means giving the forms and expression of talent credence, even if these forms are not recognized by traditional schooling practices. And finally, development means encouraging and motivating students to reach high standards of performance (Boykin, 2000). The TD Model of School Reform has six signature themes:

1. Builds on students' assets
2. Provides students with transitional support across key developmental periods in their lives
3. Engages students in constructivist and activist learning
4. Prepares students with skills for careers for the twenty-first century
5. Promotes the concept of school as community
6. Focuses on meaning and connected learning

The theoretical foundation of the TD Model was built in part by blending elements from critical pedagogy (Freire, 1973; Garcia, 1993; Giroux, 1988; hooks and West, 1991), with notions emanating from the school restructuring movement (George and Alexander, 1993; Slavin, Karweit, and Madden, 1998) and from research on the effective education of children of color (Boykin, 1994; Tharp and Gallimore, 1989).

TD interventions seek to educate the whole child. The work does not simply focus on raising students' test scores on standardized achievement measures. We seek to educate children for a vast array of intellectual, social-emotional, and transformative competencies; character building; personal fulfillment; and dual competence in the larger society as well as in their own local community. To date, CRESPAR interventions and evaluations have taken place primarily in underresourced schools serving low-income (predominantly African American) urban schools in the northeastern United States in cities such as Washington, D.C., and Baltimore, Maryland.

Conceptualizing and Using a Talent Development Evaluation Framework

Talent Development school reform interventions, like many others (see Slavin and Fashola, 1998), have been challenged to test their reform efforts against a consistent set of standards of evidence. Yet TD evaluations, as formulated by Howard University CRESPAR, are not simply scientific endeavors in search of "truth" (or more precisely "probable truths") and "solutions." They also represent social justice and critical enterprises whereby CRESPAR reform designers and implementers argue for the use of evaluation results to advocate change and restructuring for improvements in schools, especially schools serving poor, urban students. Standards of evidence for evaluations of TD projects encompass both scientific-methodological and political-activist criteria.

Evaluations of TD interventions embrace multiple purposes and perspectives that are intended to:

- Generate a more profound understanding of urban education, its students, and its contexts (knowledge development)
- Help strengthen urban students and schools (developmental evaluation)
- Provide information that will enlighten and empower those who have been oppressed by or marginalized in school systems (transformative evaluation)
- Examine the merit, worth, productivity, and value of reform efforts (accountability and outcomes evaluation)

From this perspective, our evaluations emphasize both process and outcome.

TD evaluators at times become members of the design team helping to shape intervention processes, thus blurring the conventional, and often rigid, boundaries between project designer and project evaluator. For example, TD evaluators may be involved in making decisions about the kinds of interventions that should be implemented at the school site to best meet the needs of stakeholders, as identified in earlier discussions with key stakeholder groups and from the results of various needs assessments. For us, this is not problematic, and it is actually considered an asset to evaluation planning and implementation. In these instances, TD evaluators are in a better position (in contrast to the distant evaluators) to assess process and outcomes because of their intimate knowledge of the project's components, underlying logic model, and the contexts of implementation. A distinctive feature of this integrated team approach is that individuals serving in all roles (project designer, implementer, evaluator) have a collective responsibility to and are accountable for project development, implementation, and evaluation. As members of an integrated team, TD project designers, implementers, and evaluators are all working for the same overarching agenda: enhancing the academic achievement and social-emotional competence of school-aged children, particularly those who have traditionally fared poorly in school.

As illustrated by the CRESPAR authors of the other chapters in this volume, TD evaluations and evaluators are partly accountable to the aims of the TD intervention and what happens within the intervention. Evaluation is not simply something that is done *to* the school context or reform intervention, but instead is something that is done *for* the school and its intervention efforts. Although this approach is not commonly practiced in the evaluation community, it seems a necessary paradigm when working in traditionally underserved communities. In these contexts, evaluators are not (and cannot be) neutral or benign actors that neither support nor do not support the intervention activities. This is consistent with Greene's proposition (2003) that the evaluation (and evaluator) inevitably advances some values, but not others, and therefore serves some interests, but not others. TD evaluators often take a stance through their involvement with program design (for example, assisting in clarifying important and contextually responsive program objectives and identifying important and contextually relevant outcomes that should be recognized by program planners and implementers). TD evaluators, like all other evaluators, make a difference in the settings in which they work, changing them in some important and, it is hoped, constructive ways.

In conceptualizing our framework for evaluating TD interventions, we were informed by the lessons learned over the past three decades as the evaluation field blossomed. Our work has incorporated some of the major tenets of collaborative (Greene, 1988; Patton, 1997), participatory (Cousins and Earl, 1995; Cousins and Whitmore, 1998; King, 1998), responsive (Abma and Stake, 2001; Stake, 1975; House, 2001), deliberative (House and Howe, 2000; Greene, 2000), and culturally competent (Frierson, Hood, and Hughes, 2002), multicultural (Kirkhart, 1995), and inclusive (Mertens, 1999) evaluation approaches. In addition, our thinking about evaluating urban reform interventions has been informed by the myriad social, behavioral, and political factors affecting urban school districts. Many of the problems encountered when working within urban school settings (such as diversity issues, organizational and political constraints, and conflicting priorities) are experienced by individuals working with other community-based interventions, particularly in communities serving poor and underserved populations. Therefore, the conceptual, methodological, and strategic issues brought to bear in TD evaluations also have implications for substantive areas far beyond the field of education.

Five overlapping themes are central to the design and implementation of TD evaluations:

- Engaging stakeholders
- Co-construction
- Cultural and contextual relevance
- Responsiveness
- Triangulation of conceptual and methodological perspectives

In Howard University's CRESPAR's evaluation efforts, all or a combination of these features lay the foundation for how an evaluation is planned, carried out, and used.

Engaging Stakeholders. Stakeholder involvement has long been an expectation of good evaluation practice, as stipulated in the evaluation standards of the Joint Committee on Standards for Educational Evaluation (1994). A commitment to engaging stakeholders is central to TD evaluations.

Key stakeholders must be engaged in authentic ways throughout the entire evaluation. Obtaining genuine stakeholder engagement is a complex and labor-intensive task, especially when working in poor, diverse communities. Issues related to the identification and prioritization of relevant stakeholders, gaining access to and getting the cooperation of the different stakeholder groups (students, parents, teachers, and other school personnel), framing the right questions for particular stakeholder groups, and implementing an appropriate methodology are evaluation challenges that can be significantly addressed through engaging and collaborating with key stakeholders.

Several evaluators (for example, Chelimsky, 1998; Mertens, 1999; Weiss, 1998) have discussed the challenge of meaningfully involving marginalized groups in evaluation activities. When individuals in minority communities feel marginalized or powerless, issues of power relations (real or perceived), status, and social class differentials between the evaluators and the target population can impede the stakeholder engagement process. In our work, we have found that many parents of the urban students being served had experienced negative or even traumatic occurrences with the school system during their own youth, and as a result, they often feel antagonistic or apathetic toward school personnel and others associated with the schooling enterprise, such as educational design teams and evaluators. This presents a vexing problem when trying to collect evaluative data. Respect and trustworthiness are important factors that are taken into consideration when minority groups are considering the level of cooperation (or lack thereof) they will offer to an evaluator. Providing key stakeholders, especially those who traditionally have had less powerful roles in discussions of urban school reform, opportunities to have voice can do much to minimize problems related to unequal distribution of power and status differentials. TD evaluators can best accomplish this by giving stakeholders multiple opportunities to ask questions, critique their efforts, and provide input in various ways. This also helps to garner the needed trust and respect from stakeholders once they know that their input is wanted, valued, and, to the extent possible, incorporated into the evaluation activities.

As CRESPAR evaluators, we (along with the field implementers) begin our work by having multiple meetings with key stakeholder groups in an effort to obtain genuine buy-in to the TD philosophy and our intervention and evaluation efforts. During these meetings, we ask, we listen, we discuss, and we record. We ask stakeholders for their suggestions and, to the extent feasible, infuse their input directly into the TD activities, both programmatic and evaluative. We attempt to get to know the school—its students, staff, parents, and surrounding community—prior to the implementation of any interventions and evaluations. TD evaluators enter the urban school contexts being studied gently, respectfully, and with a willingness to listen and learn in order to plan and implement evaluations better. As some of the cases studies discussed in this volume illustrate, stakeholders' engagement varies with the nature and scope of the project under consideration.

Co-Construction. Related to stakeholder engagement is the notion of co-construction, a major feature of the TD model. Co-construction is defined as evaluators' collaborating and forming genuine partnerships with key urban school stakeholder groups (educators, school administrators, students, families, and communities) and TD project designers and implementers in order to conceptualize, implement, and evaluate school reform efforts in a manner that is responsive to the school's context. Co-construction, by necessity, involves a redistribution of power, assuming a kind of equality among different stakeholders. It also seeks to democratize the evaluation process by lessening the implicit, and sometimes explicit, power dynamics between evaluators and project stakeholders. The first facilitator of co-construction is buy-in to the TD intervention and evaluation activities (Carroll, LaPoint, and Tyler, 2001). The foundation for obtaining stakeholder buy-in should be laid during the initial process of stakeholder engagement. Co-construction is not a hurried or easy process; it takes considerable time in an effort to craft a shared vision between TD evaluators and urban school stakeholders. It is our contention that co-constructed efforts will result in a sense of ownership of the TD efforts by key stakeholders, which is essential in the face of rapidly changing leadership often evident in urban schools.

Co-construction, as described by CRESPAR inquirers, is a process of respecting the social and cultural dynamics of students, families, teachers, and other school personnel that affect learning to ensure that these stakeholders have authentic input in the programmatic and evaluative efforts (Jagers and Carroll, 2002; Carroll, LaPoint, and Tyler, 2001). This is in sharp contrast to other evaluation protocols that are essentially activities transported from one school to another. Although CRESPAR implementers and evaluators do enter a school setting with prestructured activities, modules, programs, and evaluation designs, these materials are openly shared with target school site administrators, staff, family members, and others who bring their perspective and offer guidance on how to customize these interventions for their particular school site and community (Carroll, LaPoint, and Tyler, 2001).

Co-construction is seen as both an extended form and an application of collaborative research; it represents an extension of the participatory approaches (Cousins and Earl, 1995; Cousins and Whitmore, 1998) espoused in the evaluation field. Participatory evaluation implies that when doing an evaluation, researchers, facilitators, or evaluators collaborate in some way with the individuals, groups, or communities who have a decided stake in the program (Cousins and Whitmore, 1998). From our perspective, co-construction is broader in scope than participatory evaluation, and it involves authentic inquirer-stakeholder collaboration. This takes into consideration issues of power, status, culture, and context in the collaboration process. Clearly, our co-construction can be effective only to the extent that school stakeholders are adequately informed about the TD evaluation process and TD evaluators have a keen understanding of the urban school—its students, families, teachers, administrators, and micro- and macrocontext.

TD co-construction efforts stand in contrast to traditional evaluation approaches where, in isolation, the evaluators frame the problem statement, evaluation questions, and evaluation methods or where stakeholders, at best, are consulted in the early part of evaluation planning to help define the focus of the evaluation, and, maybe, at the last phase to help the evaluator interpret data for dissemination and use. In such situations, the evaluator dominates the power relations. The co-construction framework calls for the evaluator and key school stakeholders to be ongoing partners and collaborators, jointly framing questions, methodologies, and strategies for dissemination of findings. Clearly, evaluation findings are more likely to be useful if the school stakeholders are treated as partners throughout the evaluation process (McCall, Groark, Strauss, and Johnson, 1995).

Within a co-construction framework, each major stakeholder group has the potential to offer something valuable throughout the entire evaluation process. CRESPAR inquirers have documented the heuristic and transformative value of the co-construction process for urban school stakeholders far beyond the evaluation itself (Carroll, LaPoint, and Tyler, 2001). For example, it has been noted that through co-construction with CRESPAR staff, urban school stakeholders may benefit by acquiring empowering knowledge, attitudes, and skills that can be transferred and used in other life areas in the present and in the future—for example:

- Students can use co-construction to become involved in school governance and to make the transition to school-to-career opportunities such as college, technical training, and the workplace.
- Family members, often alienated and marginalized from schools, can transfer knowledge and skills learned in co-construction to get more involved in school governance and community organizations.
- Teachers, administrators, and staff can use co-construction for increasing their involvement at the school's district level and in settings outside schools.

In TD evaluations, urban school stakeholders have input into framing evaluation questions, developing instruments, collecting data, interpreting findings, and using and disseminating the findings. This co-construction process has methodological benefits. To the extent that CRESPAR evaluators engage in open and honest dialogue with key stakeholders about what is needed to ensure fidelity to the implementation and evaluations of TD activities and these stakeholders have a meaningful role in co-constructing these efforts, they are less likely to create barriers that might jeopardize the fidelity of the evaluation process.

Cultural and Contextual Relevance. Attention to culture and context is essential to the TD evaluation framework. Although numerous definitions of *culture* can be found in the literature, a common description includes the shared values, traditions, norms, customs, arts, history, folklore, and institutions of a group of people. Psychologists have come to realize that individuals are not mere pawns or victims of culture; rather, they are "cognizers," appraisers, and interpreters of culture (Segall, Lonner, and Berry, 1998). Therefore, culture is not something that is outside individuals, where it influences their behavior; it is "an intersubjective reality through which worlds are known, created, and experienced" (Miller, 1997, p. 103). Cultural competence has been described more specifically as having a set of skills that allows one to increase one's understanding and appreciation of cultural differences and similarities within, among, and between groups and having a willingness to draw on community values, traditions, and customs (Schinke and Cole, 1992). The issue of culture and cultural competence in evaluation has been discussed in various domains including education (Boykin, 1994; Ladson-Billings, 1994; Delpit, 1995; Dilworth, 1992; Frierson, Hood, and Hughes, 2002; Hood, 1998; Shade, Kelly, and Oberg, 1997); counseling and mental health (Arrendondo, 1998; Rogler, 1989; Sue, Arrendondo, and McDavis, 1992); health, social, and human services (Lecca, 1998); and alcohol prevention (Gilbert, 1992; Moran, 1992; Robinson, 1992).

Culture should be an essential aspect of any meaningful urban school programmatic, evaluation, and policy agenda. It is a critical factor for better understanding the content and context of strategies for improving the learning systems of minority students (Jagers and Carroll, 2002). School reform efforts that strive for educational equity and excellence are likely to fail unless they are meaningfully linked to the students' and their communities' unique cultures. In order to combat students', parents', communities', and school personnel's indifference or hostility toward school reform, intervention efforts must be constructed in a manner that is consistent with the cultural background of the target population and responsive to their needs.

Context, a broader term from our perspective, includes the combination of factors (including culture) accompanying the implementation and evaluation of a project that might influence its results, including geographical location, timing, political and social climate, economic conditions, and other things going on at the same time as the project. It includes the totality of the environment in which the project takes place. In our framework, the terms *culture* and *context* are used interchangeably to draw attention to essential aspects of the stakeholders' physical, psychological, and psychosocial world that have critical influences on them. In TD evaluations, attending to issues of culture and context involves both science and art. There is the science of obtaining credible and useful data and the art of comprehending meanings and understandings within an appropriate cultural or contextual perspective. This is akin to Lincoln's notion (1991) of the art of cultural analysis and the art of dealing with people who are different from ourselves.

Rogler (1989) views culturally sensitive research as taking place through a "continuing and open-ended series of substantive and methodological insertions and adaption designed to mesh the process inquiry with the cultural characteristics of the group being studied" (p. 296). Moran (1992) stresses that to be culturally sensitive, a researcher needs to understand the meanings of the institutions, values, religious ideals, habits of thinking, artistic expressions, and patterns of social and interpersonal relationships that influence the lives of the members of the community in which the research is to take place. We embrace all of these aspects in the conceptualization and implementation of urban school reform evaluations.

Hood (1998, 2001) argues that a shared lived experience could and possibly should be accepted as being important and valuable in the evaluation of programs serving members of racial minority groups. He adds that evaluators of color are more likely to have direct experiences with their own racial and cultural group that may inform their evaluation of programs serving this group. As African American evaluators working in predominantly African American urban school settings, CRESPAR evaluators are keenly aware of and sensitive to many of the contextual and cultural issues relevant to the lives of the children and other family members being served. We bring a different set of experiences to the urban school context than do our white counterparts. Our shared racial and ethnic background increases our ability to engage stakeholders and better understand the verbal, as well as nonverbal, behaviors of the individuals being observed.

Although there are clearly characteristics that TD evaluators generally do not share with the populations being served (for example, education level and socioeconomic background), our shared racial and ethnic background still has incremental value. Hood (2001) noted that when evaluators and participants are of similar ethnic and racial background, less time will be required in translating the cultural nuances and nonverbal communications associated with observations, conducting interviews, and interpretations that go beyond quantitative indictors of what the program appears to be. As culturally competent evaluators, we must also be self-reflective and open to examining our own assumptions and stereotypes about urban schools and their stakeholders.

CRESPAR evaluators, like numerous other scholars (Hood, 2001; Frierson, Hood, and Hughes, 2002; Robinson, 1992; Stevens, 2000), argue that culturally competent research is best done by qualified representatives of the culture being served. However, we recognize that this may not always be practical or feasible given the relatively small proportion of practicing evaluators of color or individuals from underrepresented groups pursuing graduate education and careers in evaluation. In instances where evaluators are not representatives of the culture being studied, it is essential that these individuals acquire a fundamental knowledge of the cultural norms and experiences of the individuals under consideration. This can be achieved by using individuals familiar with the group being studied as informants, interpreters, or critical friends to the evaluation. Also, evaluators who are not familiar with the cultural groups being studied should engage in a process of ongoing self-reflection so that they become acutely aware of their own cultural values, assumptions, prejudices, and stereotypes and how these may affect their evaluation practice within the particular setting.`

At CRESPAR, our efforts to integrate cultural and contextual relevance in TD evaluations occur in a myriad of ways. We seek a genuine understanding of the urban school community before implementing any interventions. Through orientation meetings, informal discussions, ongoing group discussions with key stakeholders, focus groups, on-site community meetings with school stakeholders, feedback sessions, as well as preintervention needs assessments, we learn much about the school and its staff, students, parents, the surrounding community, and district-level issues (such as demands and politics). Sometimes the information gathered through these strategies enhances the cultural accuracy of the TD intervention and provides insight for planning and fine-tuning interventions. Engaging stakeholders in ongoing dialogue and co-construction also brings about more culturally relevant evaluations by helping the evaluators to become more attuned to the stakeholders' priorities and lived experiences.

Much discussion related to cultural and contextual relevance centers around the evaluator's engaging the stakeholder into the project (a unidirectional stance). We also argue that evaluators can gain much when they directly involve themselves into the life of the community being served (bidirectional stance). TD evaluators learn a great deal through active involvement in the urban school and its community. For example, TD evaluators sometimes attend school fundraisers, family nights, and other school-related activities. These activities are done not for the purpose of gathering evaluation data but to achieve a more intimate understanding of the school culture and context and to increase stakeholders' level of respect and trust for the evaluators and, ultimately, the evaluation process. In other words, a central part of TD evaluations is also related to building relationships and bonding with key stakeholders throughout the evaluation process.

Responsiveness. Another central and related theme of TD evaluations is responsiveness, a concept introduced by Robert Stake (1987). Responsiveness is closely related to the other TD evaluation framework features of engaging stakeholders and co-construction. TD evaluations embrace the underlying philosophy of responsiveness found in the literature (Abma and Stake, 2001; House, 2001; Hood, 2001; Stake, 1987). A major aspect of responsiveness is respecting, honoring, attending to, and representing stakeholders' perspectives (House, 2001). House urged responsive evaluators to "look away from the statistics tests and toward the people whose programs were under review" (pp. 28–29). In TD evaluations, responsiveness is actualized by considering, as a point of departure, urban school stakeholders' perspectives prior to planning, implementing, and evaluating any interventions. Furthermore, we revisit these issues throughout the entire process to ensure that, to the extent possible, we continue to be responsive to stakeholders' needs in an environment of change and competing demands. Using a responsive approach to evaluation helps us to focus on the ways we ought to think and act in our evaluation practice.

TD evaluators share the evaluation information with the urban school stakeholders in ways that maximize relevance for developing and implementing strategies for improving various outcomes (for example, students' academic, social, emotional, and cultural development and family and community involvement). This is consistent with Hood's view (2001) that a responsive evaluator orchestrates an evaluation that culminates in a reporting of findings that comes closest to letting the audience see, hear, and touch the essence of the program and how it is functioning.

Triangulation of Perspectives. A final central theme of TD evaluations is triangulation of perspectives. Triangulation generally involves the use of both quantitative and qualitative data in a single study or in multiple studies of a sustained program of research on a particular phenomenon in order to increase the scope of confidence in the inquiry findings. Triangulation involving mixed methods is certainly not a new approach in social research (Campbell and Fiske, 1959; Jick, 1979; McGrath, 1982), and it has been extensively discussed in the evaluation field (Caracelli and Greene, 1997; Greene and Caracelli, 1997; Greene, Caracelli, and Graham, 1989; Greene and McClintock, 1985). Increasingly, more evaluations are relying on mixed methods, recognizing that both approaches (quantitative and qualitative) are valuable and have something unique to offer. In fact, in a fairly recent interview published in *The Evaluation Exchange* (Harvard Family Research Project, 2002), Patton indicated that he considered the "end to the qualitative-quantitative debate" to be one of the top four or five "breakthrough ideas" over the past fifteen years that has helped define and influence modern evaluation practice.

At Howard CRESPAR, we triangulate our evaluations in multiple ways:

Investigator triangulation—having a research team with shared interests in a topic and diverse perspectives and areas of expertise regarding the topic (for example, a multidisciplinary study team including a sociologist, anthropologist, social worker, and psychologist)

Multiple operationalism—using different ways to measure a single concept in an effort to gather multiple perspectives and a deeper understanding of the issue (for example, measuring student achievement in terms of standardized test scores, grades, and teachers' ratings)

Methodological triangulation—using more than one research method or data collection technique that may assess different dimensions of a problem (for example, quantitative and qualitative)

Target person triangulation—collecting data from more than one person on a particular issue (for example, gathering student behavioral data from students, family members, and teachers)

Analysis triangulation—using more than one strategy or statistical technique to analyze the same data

Triangulating our TD evaluations supports the strengths of interpretations and conclusions drawn. Traditionally, triangulation is used to obtain convergence, comprehensiveness, or corroboration of findings (that is, a "single truth"). For TD evaluators, it is about inclusiveness of perspectives and validity through this inclusiveness. As a result, our triangulated approaches to TD evaluations may yield many answers to a single question, which can generate deeper and broader insights into the issue under consideration.

Challenges in Implementing TD Evaluations

Planning and implementing TD evaluations in urban school settings, like other community-based research efforts, are certainly not without challenges. Many urban schools lack a culture that values and supports change, evidence-based practices, and ongoing inquiry, especially when these activities are designed and implemented by outsiders such as university-based researchers. Challenges occur at the TD level, the school level, the community level, the district level, and a combination of these.

Timing is often a problem. TD evaluations are both time-consuming and labor intensive, with much emphasis placed on developing alliances and co-constructing with schools and communities, conducting needs assessments, attending to issues of culture and context, and using inclusive methodological perspectives. Some TD inquirers argue that a full year is needed to conduct start-up activities such as learning about a school's physical structure and functioning, the school's personnel and stakeholders, and the school's culture and climate and to collectively plan interventions and collect baseline data (Carroll, LaPoint, and Tyler, 2001). Often, funding agencies are not receptive to such a lengthy start-up period.

Two other inherent challenges in conducting TD evaluations relate to (1) diversity issues and power relations and (2) mismatched and conflicted priorities. Our urban school reform interventions and evaluations take place in an environment characterized by diverse individuals and groups. Diversity exists among and between CRESPAR staff and the urban school stakeholders along several important dimensions, such as social class, education level, gender, status, and needs. These differences can result in real or perceived power differentials among various groups, such as between CRESPAR staff and urban school stakeholders, teachers and school administrators, or teachers and family members of the urban school students. If this is not recognized and effectively dealt with (for example, through stakeholder engagement and ongoing dialogue), difficulties can arise when CRESPAR evaluators begin to work with and gain support from certain stakeholder groups. The benefits of crafting a shared vision through stakeholder engagement and co-construction have far-reaching effects by giving school personnel, students, family members, and community members voice and choice.

Another diversity challenge occurs when racial and ethnic differences exist wherein students and their families are African American and the urban school's teachers and staff are not African American. This can result in cultural conflicts and misunderstandings. Much has been written about the cultural conflicts in the classroom and teaching "other people's" children (see, for example, Delpit, 1995; Lee, 1997, 2000). From our perspective, these cultural clashes can have a deleterious effect on the implementation and evaluation of our interventions. For example, when an observer (say, a white female teacher) does not share her students' racial and ethnic background, she has little shared lived experience to draw on when making attributions about students' attitudes and behaviors. As a result, teachers can misinterpret, misjudge, or mislabel certain characteristics of their students. This can become a troublesome issue for evaluators who heavily rely on teachers' judgments in identifying students placed at risk for academic failure and in making referrals for TD academic support services. In such cases, target person triangulation and multiple operationalism are essential.

Another pressing challenge relates to mismatched or conflicted priorities among and between CRESPAR staff and urban school key stakeholder groups. CRESPAR staff, teachers, administrators, students and their families, and funders may all have different sets of priorities in relation to what they ultimately want from TD interventions. For example, the funders are not so much concerned with the extent to which the funded intervention worked (or did not work) for a particular group of students at a particular school. Ultimately, their major priority is often that of having sufficient evidence that will justify scaling up or replicating successful projects in other settings. As a result, funders are increasingly pushing for rigorous scientific, controlled experiments with randomization to demonstrate impact. Although we maintain that experimental designs are far superior to nonexperimental designs for assessing questions of impact as they represent the best way to rule out threats to internal validity, such designs are not easily implemented in the ever-changing environment of poor urban school settings. Students' major priorities generally center around being promoted through the grades, being able to graduate on time, being eligible to attend college or acquire further technical training, being able to enlist in the military, or having marketable skills for gainful employment. They often want quick fixes to complicated problems like academic failure. The priorities of district- and school-level administrators and teachers often focus very narrowly on improving test performance, particularly under the NCLB Act. In all of these instances, our challenge becomes finding that delicate balance among the competing evaluative demands and responding to them from a perspective that is contextually and culturally responsive.

The politics of the NCLB legislation have major implications for how evaluators of educational interventions will conceptualize, implement, and present their work. The definitions of scientifically based research written into the NCLB law use as exemplar experiments, meta-analyses, and randomized trials. There is much ongoing debate within the evaluation community about this narrow view of research (as reflected in dialogue on EVAL TALK, the American Evaluation Association's discussion listserv). Through such discussions, it is evident that some American Evaluation Association members support this approach, arguing that randomized methods and, in limited circumstances, quasi-experimental methods are absolutely essential to understanding what works and where. Other members do not dispute the assertion that randomized experimental designs are important; however, they argue that in many instances, this approach cannot be properly implemented given the complexity of contextual factors inherent in many school settings, particularly diverse, low-income urban schools. Jolly (2002) stresses that evaluators have to accept the possibility that they may have "missing bricks" of foundational knowledge when studying underrepresented groups and the settings in which these groups operate. At CRESPAR, we argue that the selection and use of evaluation methods should be guided by the project and evaluation objectives, what is to be considered appropriate evidence within the particular school context, and how this evidence will be linked to improvement efforts and other decisions about using evaluation results. This is reflected in our support for a triangulated perspective in relation to both programmatic and evaluative efforts since context factors that often tell the "whole story" (and therefore address those "missing bricks") of the intervention and evaluation cannot be neatly compressed into the traditional experimental and controlled group pretest-posttest design.

Recommendations for Conducting Evaluations in Urban Settings

Based on our experiences at Howard University CRESPAR, we offer the following recommendations to evaluators who work in urban school settings or other environments serving low-income, diverse populations:

• *Front-load efforts.* The complexity of urban school communities makes it critical that persons working in these environments understand the project's context. Therefore, prior to the implementation of any school-based interventions or evaluation activities, project staff must spend ample time getting to know the urban school or organizational setting—including its students, families, staff, and the micro- and macroeducational and political context.

• *Engage the stakeholders in meaningful ways throughout the evaluation process.* This can be done through various ways, such as holding small group meetings, focus groups, and individualized discussions with key stakeholders to deeply understand their perspectives. Evaluators should ask about, listen to, and hear stakeholders' issues, concerns, and suggestions. Stakeholder engagement must be authentic and not superficial.

• *Co-construct inquiry activities.* Evaluators should give stakeholders an opportunity to assist with the framing of evaluation questions, instrument design, data collection, interpretation of findings, and dissemination of results. To the extent feasible, stakeholders' suggestions and feedback should be integrated into evaluation planning, implementation, dissemination efforts, and use of findings.

• *Give back to the community in tangible and intangible ways.* This can be readily accomplished by conducting evaluations that are responsive to stakeholders' needs, desires, and context and by presenting findings in ways that are meaningful and serve the information needs of the various stakeholder groups.

• *Ensure that all evaluation staff working in urban communities are culturally competent.* Evaluation staff must deeply understand, appreciate, and value the culture and context they are working within in the urban school setting. Evaluation activities must be constructed in a manner that is congruent with the cultural background of the individuals being served.

• *Treat all urban stakeholders with respect and dignity.* In accordance with good ethical practice, as espoused by the American Evaluation Association's Guiding Principles for Evaluators, evaluators must treat urban stakeholders humanely, fairly, and with dignity and due regard for their welfare.

• *Be patient and understanding, and have a high tolerance for ambiguity and change.* Individuals working in urban school environments must be cognizant of the harsh reality that these schools often function in a crisis mode: inadequate funding and resources, staff turnover, changing priorities, and competing agendas can have a powerful influence on the planning, implementation, and evaluation of interventions. Individuals working in these environments must be able to make adjustments to these changing dynamics without becoming overly discouraged, unappreciative, or insensitive to the challenges facing the urban school environment. In other words, individuals working in settings that are in a constant state of flux must be flexible and learn to adjust to the changing milieu.

Conclusions

Working in urban school environments and other diverse community-based settings requires evaluators to have a diverse toolbox of knowledge and skills. The TD framework is grounded in the themes of stakeholder engagement, co-construction, responsiveness, cultural and contextual relevance, and triangulation of perspectives. We believe that this inclusive and triangulated approach to evaluation can bring more credibility, integrity, and fidelity to TD efforts. Inclusive evaluation, as noted by American Evaluation Association's past president Donna Mertens (1999), has the potential to contribute to an enhanced ability to assert truth, objectivity, credibility, validity, and rigor in the sense that ignored or misrepresented views are included.

TD evaluations can provide K–12 school administrators with the data they need to make informed and data-driven decisions about best practices for urban students who have traditionally not fared well in school. Of course, it must be acknowledged that with every evaluation looms the possibility of uncovering bad news. Notwithstanding, we also recognize that it can be equally instructive to learn what does not work and with whom as it is to determine what does work. In other words, good evaluations can raise as many questions as they answer. Through our efforts at Howard University CRESPAR, we have made some significant progress in many areas (for example, engaging and building relationships with key urban school stakeholders, co-constructing intervention and evaluation efforts), whereas in other areas, we continue to wrestle with vexing concerns related to the dynamic and complex nature of urban schools. The CRESPAR case studies presented in this volume attest to both our successes and challenges.

References

Abma, T. A., and Stake, R. E. "Stake's Responsive Evaluation: Core Ideas and Evaluation." In J. C. Greene and T. A. Abma (eds.), *Responsive Evaluation.* New Directions for Evaluation, no. 92. San Francisco: Jossey-Bass, 2001.

American Psychological Association. *Bringing to Scale Educational Innovation and School Reform: Partnerships in Urban Education.* Conference proceedings, June 26–28, 1997. Washington, D.C., American Psychological Association, 1997.

Arrendondo, P. "Integrating Multicultural Counseling Competencies and Universal Helping Conditions in Culture-Specific Contexts." *Counseling Psychologist,* 1998, *26,* 592–601.

Boykin, A. W. "Harvesting Talent and Culture: African American Children and Educational Reform." In R. Rossi (ed.), *Schools and Students at Risk.* New York: Teachers College Press, 1994.

Boykin, A. W. "The Talent Development Model of Schooling: Placing Students at Promise for Academic Success." *Journal of Education for Students Placed at Risk,* 2000, *5*(1/2), 3–25.

Boykin, A. W., and Slavin, R. (guest eds.). "CRESPAR Findings (1994–1999): In Memory of John H. Hollifield, Jr." *Journal of Education for Students Placed at Risk,* 2000, *5*(1/2), 1–211 (special issue).

Campbell, D. T., and Fiske, D. W. "Convergent and Discriminant Validation by the Multitrait-Multi-Method Matrix." *Psychological Bulletin,* 1959, *56,* 81–105.

Caracelli, V. J., and Greene, J. C. "Crafting Mixed-Method Evaluation Design." In J. C. Greene and V. Caracelli (eds.), *Advances in Mixed-Method Evaluation: The Challenges and Benefits of Integrating Diverse Paradigms.* New Directions for Program Evaluation, no. 74. San Francisco: Jossey-Bass, 1997.

Carroll, G., LaPoint, V., and Tyler, K. "Co-Construction: A Facilitator for School Reform in School, Community and University Partnerships." *Journal of Negro Education,* 2001, *70*(1/2), 38–58.

Chelimsky, E. "The Role of Experience in Formulating Theories of Evaluation Practice." *American Journal of Evaluation,* 1998, *19*(1), 35–56.

Chelimsky, E., and Shadish, W. R. (eds.). *Evaluation for the Twenty-First Century:* A *Handbook.* Thousand Oaks, Calif.: Sage, 1997.

Comer, J. *School Power.* New York: Free Press, 1980.

Comer, J., Haynes, N. M., Joyner, E. T., and Ben-Avie, M. *Rallying the Whole Village: The Comer Process for Reforming Education.* New York: Teachers College Press, 1996.

Cousins, J. B., and Earl, L. M. (eds.). *Participatory Evaluation in Education: Studies in Evaluation Use and Organizational Learning.* Bristol, Pa.: Falmer, 1995.

Cousins, J. B., and Whitmore, E. "Framing Participatory Evaluation." In E. Whitmore (ed.), New *Directions for Evaluation,* no. 80. San Francisco: Jossey-Bass, 1998.

Delpit, L. *Other People's Children: Cultural Conflict in the Classroom.* New York: New York Press, 1995.

Dilworth, M. (ed.). *Diversity in Teacher Education: New Expectations.* San Francisco: Jossey-Bass, 1992.

Engelbrecht, L., and Rashid, H. "The Learners Placed At Risk Project (LEAPAR): A Framework for Implementing the Talent Development Model in South African Schools." Paper presented at the annual conference of the American Educational Research Association, San Diego, Calif., Apr. 2002.

Freire, P. *Pedagogy of the Oppressed.* New York: Seabury, 1973.

Frierson, H. T., Hood, S., and Hughes, G. "Strategies That Address Culturally Responsive Evaluation." In *The 2002 User-Friendly Handbook for Project Evaluation.* Arlington, Va.: National Science Foundation, 2002.

Garcia, E. E. "Language, Culture and Education." *Review of Research in Education,* 1993, *19,* 51–98.

George, P. S., and Alexander, W. M. *The Exemplary Middle School.* Orlando, Fla.: Harcourt, 1993.

Gilbert, M. J. "Conducting Culturally Competent Alcohol Prevention Research in Ethnic Communities." In P. A. Langton (ed.), *The Challenge of Participatory Research: Preventing Alcohol-Related Problems in Ethnic Communities.* Washington, D.C.: U.S. Department of Health and Human Services, Substance Abuse and Mental Health Services Administration, 1992.

Giroux, H. *Teachers as Intellectuals: A Critical Pedagogy for Practical Learning.* Westport, Conn.: Bergin and Garvey, 1988.

Greene, J. C. "Communication of Results and Utilization in Participatory Program Evaluation." *Evaluation and Program Planning,* 1988, *11,* 341–351.

Greene, J. C. "Challenges in Practicing Deliberative Democratic Evaluation." In K. E. Ryan and L. DeStefano (eds.), *Evaluation as a Democratic Process: Promoting Inclusion, Dialogue, and Deliberation.* New Directions for Evaluation, no. 85. San Francisco: Jossey-Bass, 2000.

Greene, J. C. "Evaluation as Engagement with Difference—In Service of the Public Good." Keynote address at the Howard University Evaluation Training Institute, Washington, D.C., June 16, 2003.

Greene, J. C., and Caracelli, V. J. (eds.). *Advances in Mixed-Method Evaluation: The Challenges and Benefits of Integrating Diverse Paradigms.* New Directions for Program Evaluation, no. 74. San Francisco: Jossey-Bass, 1997.

Greene, J. C., Caracelli, V. J., and Graham, W. F. "Toward a Conceptual Framework for Mixed-Method Evaluation Designs." *Educational Evaluation and Policy Analysis,* 1989, *11,* 255–274.

Greene, J., and McClintock, C. "Triangulation in Evaluation: Design and Analysis Issues." *Evaluation Review,* 1985, *9,* 523–545.

Guba, E. G., and Lincoln, Y. S. *Effective Evaluation.* San Francisco: Jossey-Bass, 1981.

Harvard Family Research Project of the Harvard Graduate School of Education. "A Conversation with Michael Quinn Patton." *The Evaluation Exchange,* 2002 (Spring), *8*(1), 10–11.

Hood, S. "Responsive Evaluation Amistad Style: Perspectives of One African American Evaluator." In R. Davis (ed.), *Proceedings of the Stake Symposium on Educational Evaluation.* Urbana-Champaign: University of Illinois, 1998.

Hood, S. "Nobody Knows My Name: In Praise of African American Evaluators Who Were Responsive." In J. C. Greene and T. A. Abma (eds.), *Responsive Evaluation.* New Directions for Evaluation, no. 92. San Francisco: Jossey-Bass, 2001.

hooks, b., and West, C. *Breaking Bread: Insurgent Black Intellectual Life.* Boston: South End Press, 1991.

Hopfenberg, W. S., and Levin, H. M. *The Accelerated School Resource Guide.* San Francisco: Jossey-Bass, 1993.

House, E. R. "Responsive Evaluation (and Its Influence on Deliberative Democratic Evaluation)." In J. C. Greene and T. A. Abma (eds.), *Responsive Evaluation.* New Directions for Evaluation, no. 92. San Francisco: Jossey-Bass, 2001.

House, E. R., and Howe, K. R. "Deliberative Democratic Evaluation." In K. E. Ryan and L. DeStefano (eds.), *Evaluation as a Democratic Process: Promoting Inclusion, Dialogue, and Deliberation.* New Directions for Evaluation, no. 85. San Francisco: Jossey-Bass, 2000.

Jagers, R. J. (guest ed.). "Samplings from Howard University CRESPAR." *Journal of Negro Education,* 2001, 70(1/2), 1–113 (special issue).

Jagers, R. J., and Carroll, G. "Issues in Educating African American Children and Youth." In S. Stringfield and D. Land (eds.), *Educating At-Risk Students.* Chicago: University of Chicago Press, 2002.

Jick, T. D. "Mixing Qualitative and Quantitative Methods: Triangulation in Action." *Administrative Science Quarterly,* 1979, 24, 602–611.

Johnson, R. *Using Data to Close the Achievement Gap: How to Measure Equity in Our Schools.* Thousand Oaks, Calif.: Corwin Press, 2002.

Joint Committee on Standards for Educational Evaluation. *The Program Evaluation Standards: How to Assess Evaluations of Educational Programs.* (2nd ed.) Thousand Oaks, Calif.: Sage, 1994.

Jolly, E. J. "On the Quest for Cultural Context in Evaluation: Non Ceteris Paribus." In *The National Science Foundation, The Cultural Context of Educational Evaluation: A Native American Perspective.* Arlington, Va.: Directorate for Education and Human Resources, Division of Research, Evaluation and Communication, 2002.

King, J. A. "Making Sense of Participatory Evaluation Practice." In E. Whitmore (ed.), *Understanding and Practicing Participatory Evaluation.* New Directions for Evaluation, no. 80. San Francisco: Jossey-Bass, 1998.

Kirkhart, K. E. "Seeking Multicultural Validity: A Postcard from the Road." *Evaluation Practice,* 1995, 16, 1–12.

Kozol, J. *Savage Inequalities.* New York: Crown, 1991.

Ladson-Billings, G. *Dreamkeepers: Successful Teachers of African American Children.* San Francisco: Jossey-Bass, 1994.

Lecca, P. J. (ed.). *Cultural Competency in Health, Social, and Human Services: Directions for the Twenty-First Century.* New York: Garland, 1998.

Lee, C. D. "Bridging Home and School Literacies: A Model of Culturally Responsive Teaching." In J. Flood, S. B. Heath, and D. Lapp (eds.), *A Handbook for Literacy Educators: Research on Teaching the Communicative and Visual Arts.* New York: Macmillan, 1997.

Lee, C. D. "Signifying in the Zone of Proximal Development." In C. D. Lee and P. Smagorinsky (eds.), *Vygotskian Perspectives on Literary Research: Constructing Meaning Through Collaborative Inquiry.* Cambridge: Cambridge University Press, 2000.

Levin, H. M. "Accelerated Schools for Disadvantaged Students." *Educational Leadership,* 1987, 44(6), 19–21.

Lincoln, Y. S. "Toward a Categorical Imperative for Qualitative Research." In E. W. Eisner and A. Peshkin (eds.), *Qualitative Inquiry in Education: The Continuing Debate.* New York: Teachers College Press, 1991.

McCall, R. B., Groark, C. J., Strauss, M. S., and Johnson, C. N. "The University of Pittsburgh Office of Child Development—An Experiment in Promoting Interdisciplinary Applied Human Development." *Journal of Applied Developmental Psychology,* 1995, *6,* 593–612.

McGrath, J. "Dilemmatics: The Study of Research Choices and Dilemmas." In J. E. McGrath, J. Martin, and R. A. Kulka (eds.), *Judgment Calls in Research.* Thousand Oaks, Calif.: Sage, 1982.

Mertens, D. M. "Inclusive Evaluation: Implications of Transformative Theory for Evaluation." *American Journal of Evaluation,* 1999, *20*(1), 1–14.

Miller, J. G. "Theoretical Issues in Cultural Psychology." In J. W. Berry, Y. H. Poortinga, and J. Pandey (eds.), *Handbook of Cross-Cultural Psychology: Theory and Method.* Needham Heights, Mass.: Allyn & Bacon, 1997.

Moran, J. R. "Culturally Sensitive Alcohol Prevention Research in Ethnic Communities." In P. A. Langton (ed.), *The Challenge of Participatory Research: Preventing Alcohol-Related Problems in Ethnic Communities.* Washington, D.C.: U.S. Department of Health and Human Services, Substance Abuse and Mental Health Services Administration, 1992.

Noguera, P. "Confronting the Urban in Urban School Reform." *Urban Review,* 1996, *28*(1).

Oakes, J. "Tracking, Inequality, and the Rhetoric of Reform: Why Schools Don't Change." *Journal of Education,* 1986, *168*(1), 60–79.

Oakes, J., and Guiton, G. "Opportunity to Learn and Conception of Educational Equality." *Educational Evaluation and Policy Analysis,* 1995, *17*(3), 323–336.

Patton, M. Q. *Qualitative Evaluation and Research Methods.* Thousand Oaks, Calif.: Sage, 1990.

Patton, M. Q. *Utilization-Focused Evaluation: The New Century Text.* Thousand Oaks, Calif.: Sage, 1997.

Rashid, H. "Howard University CRESPAR/South African Initiative." *Talent Development of Students Placed At Risk Special Interest Group (SIG) Newsletter,* 2000 (Fall), *2*(1), 1, 3.

Robinson, R. G. "The Relevancy of Cultural Sensitivity in Alcohol Prevention Research in Ethnic/Racial Communities." In P. A. Langton (ed.), *The Challenge of Participatory Research: Preventing Alcohol-Related Problems in Ethnic Communities.* Washington, D.C.: U.S. Department of Health and Human Services, Substance Abuse and Mental Health Services Administration, 1992.

Rogler, L. H. "The Meaning of Culturally Sensitive Research in Mental Health." *American Journal of Psychiatry,* 1989, *146*(3), 296–303.

Rossman, G. B., and Rallis, S. F. "Critical Inquiry and Use as Action." In V. J. Caracelli and H. Preskill (eds.), *The Expanding Scope of Evaluation Use.* New Directions for Evaluation, no. 88. San Francisco: Jossey-Bass, 2000.

Schinke, S. P., and Cole, K. C. "Methodological Issues in Conducting Alcohol Abuse Prevention Research in Ethnic Communities." In P. A. Langton (ed.), *The Challenge of Participatory Research: Preventing Alcohol-Related Problems in Ethnic Communities.* Washington, D.C.: U.S. Department of Health and Human Services, Substance Abuse and Mental Health Services Administration, 1992.

Schwartz, W. "Closing the Achievement Gap: Principles for Improving the Educational Success of All Students." *ERIC Digest.* New York: ERIC Clearinghouse on Urban Education, Dec. 2001.

Segall, M. L., Lonner, W. J., and Berry, J. W. "Cross-Cultural Psychology as a Scholarly Discipline: On the Flowering of Culture in a Scholarly Discipline." *American Psychologist,* 1998, *53,* 1101–1110.

Shade, B. J., Kelly, C., and Oberg, M. *Creating Culturally Responsive Classrooms.* Washington, D.C.: American Psychological Association, 1997.

Sizer, T. *Horace's Compromise: The Dilemma of the American High School.* Boston: Houghton Mifflin, 1984.

Sizer, T. *Horace's School.* Boston: Houghton Mifflin, 1992.

Sizer, T. *Horace's Hope.* Boston: Houghton Mifflin, 1996.

Slavin, R. E., and Fashola, O. S. *Show Me the Evidence! Proven and Promising Programs for America's Schools.* Thousand Oaks, Calif.: Corwin, 1998.

Slavin, R. E., Karweit, N. L., and Madden, N. *Effective Programs for Students at Risk.* Needham Heights, Mass.: Allyn & Bacon, 1998.

Slavin, R. E., Madden, N. A., Dolan, L. J., and Wasik, B. A. *Every Child, Every School: Success for All.* Thousand Oaks, Calif.: Corwin, 1996.

Stake, R. E. *Evaluating the Arts in Education: A Responsive Approach.* Columbus, Ohio: Merrill, 1975.

Stake, R. E. "Program Evaluation, Particularly Responsive Evaluation." In G. F. Madaus, M. S. Shriven, and D. L. Stufflebeam (eds.), *Evaluation Models: Viewpoints on Educational and Human Services Evaluation.* Norwell, Mass.: Kluwer-Nijhoff, 1987.

Stevens, F. I. "Reflections and Interviews: Information Collected About Training Minority Evaluators of Math and Science Projects." In *The Cultural Context of Educational Evaluation: The Role of Minority Evaluation Professionals.* Arlington, Va.: National Science Foundation, Directorate for Education and Human Resources, 2000.

Sue, D. W., Arrendondo, P., and McDavis, R. J. "Multicultural Counseling Competencies and Standards: A Call to the Profession." *Journal of Counseling and Development,* 1992, *70,* 477–486.

Tharp, R., and Gallimore, R. *Rousing Minds to Life: Teaching, Learning and School in Social Context.* Cambridge: Cambridge University Press, 1989.

Waters, G. A. "Critical Evaluation for Education Reform." *Education Policy Analysis Archives,* 1998, *6*(30), 1–36.

Weiss, C. "Have We Learned Anything New About the Use of Evaluation?" *American Journal of Evaluation,* 1998, *19*(1), 21–34.

Whitmore, E. (ed.). *Understanding and Practicing Participatory Evaluation.* New Directions for Evaluation, no. 80. San Francisco: Jossey-Bass, 1998.

Williams, B. (ed.). *Closing the Achievement Gap: A Vision for Changing Beliefs and Practices.* Alexandria, Va.: Association for Supervision and Curriculum Development, 1996.

VERONICA G. THOMAS is coprincipal investigator of the Secondary School Project at the Center for Research on the Education of Students Placed At Risk and professor in the Department of Human Development and Psychoeducational Studies, Howard University, Washington, D.C. She is also principal investigator of the Howard University Evaluation Training Institute.

2

Selected program participants became trained assistant evaluators when a school-based family, school, and community partnership program for black students in a low-income urban high school was evaluated using Talent Development strategies.

Evaluating the Co-Construction of the Family, School, and Community Partnership Program in a Low-Income Urban High School

Velma LaPoint, Henry L. Jackson

There have been resounding national calls in the past several years to improve the academic achievement and social competence of students in public schools, especially students in low-performing K–12 schools that include low-income students of color in the nation's urban communities (Chapter One, this volume; Delpit, 2003; Boykin, 2000). Many educational stakeholders—students, teachers, administrators, and family members—have become involved in providing personal, material, and financial resources for improving student achievement and social competence in areas such as curriculum and instruction, professional development, and academic support programs (Berger, 2003; Wright and Stegelin, 2003). Community stakeholders, including elected officials, college and university representatives who work to align K–16 student knowledge and skill requirements, workplace representatives who will hire students as future employees, and funding officials of educational programs such as the federal government and foundations have also been involved in these efforts (Brotherton, 2003; Education Trust, 2003).

The work reported herein was supported by grant(s) from the Institute of Education Sciences (IES) (formerly the Office of Educational Research and Improvement), U.S. Department of Education. The findings and opinions expressed in this chapter do not necessarily reflect the position or policies of the Institute of Education Sciences or the U.S. Department of Education.

One type of student academic support program that continues to receive national attention is the school and community partnership program, including partnerships with colleges and universities (Carroll, LaPoint, and Tyler, 2001; Duffy and Dale, 2001; Maurrasse, 2001). Many stakeholders who provide program resources want to know if and how programs work, especially in times where educational needs are greater than resource availability (Posavac and Carey, 2003). Research indicates that many of these partnership programs have positive impacts on student achievement, and this includes low-income students of color in low-performing schools (Sanders, 2001; Epstein, 2001, 2002; Berger, 2003; Wright and Stegelin, 2003). Given the growth of these programs, there is a need to address program evaluation issues.

This chapter focuses on evaluating the co-construction of a school-based family, school, and community partnership program for black students in a low-income urban high school. This intervention, the Family, School, and Community Partnership Program (FSCPP), is one of several academic support programs that seek to improve student academic achievement and social competence in secondary schools in the Talent Development Secondary School Project (TDSSP) at Howard University's Center for Research on the Education of Students Placed At Risk (CRESPAR). Although there are some unique aspects in the evaluation of this school-based intervention, evaluators of the FSCPP faced issues that have implications for the general evaluation community. For example, community-based public institutions serving low-income individuals and their families often share similar characteristics and challenges. These include working with individuals and families who may be marginalized by institutional barriers of race, class, gender, age, and other factors. These barriers often serve to create various responses from individuals and their families including feelings of alienation, apathy, and inconsistent participation in intervention programs that seek to benefit them—all of which will have an effect on program evaluation.

Guiding Principles and Models

Several models and applied evaluation frameworks guided the development, implementation, and evaluation of FSCPP. CRESPAR's Talent Development Model (Boykin, 2000; Carroll, LaPoint, and Tyler, 2001), a whole school reform model that encompasses co-construction and evidenced-based practices, and the TD evaluation framework (Chapter One, this volume) were the overarching models. As one component of CRESPAR, the TDSSP develops, implements, and evaluates academic support programs for secondary school students in four areas: (1) professional development for teachers and staff; (2) academic tutoring and enrichment for students; (3) career exploration and development for students; and (4) family, school, and community partnership activities.

Two other major program models—the National Network of Partnership Schools (NNPS; Epstein, 2001, 2002) and participatory action research (PAR; Argyris and Schön, 1991)—also influenced the development of the FSCPP. The NNPS seeks to enhance the academic achievement and competence of students by integrating high-quality school reform programs with a comprehensive, evidenced-based framework of school, family, and community partnerships. The NNPS framework comprises three overlapping spheres of influence (OSI)—schools, families, and communities—that have collaborative practices to support student achievement and social competence. With students in the center of the OSI, student success is promoted through six types of school, family, and community collaborative practices (Epstein, 2001, 2002):

• Positive parenting
• Communication
• Volunteerism
• At-home learning
• Collective decision making
• Collaboration with the community

Principles of the PAR model were also used (Argyris and Schön, 1991). PAR is an empirically grounded model for social inquiry that views participants and researchers as partners in the investigation of events within real-life contexts of program design, implementation, and evaluation. PAR mandates that ongoing, formative evaluations of school reform activities be conducted throughout the stages of program development and implementation and that all stakeholders should be engaged early and often in program evaluation (Cousins and Earl, 1995; Torres, Preskill, and Piontek, 1996).

Selected evaluation principles and their application was the fourth body of information used in the FSCPP, notably its evaluation. Brandon (1998) uses several terms that TDSSP staff have adopted to describe evaluation principles and their applications. For example, TDSSP evaluators use practical participatory evaluation, which is the process in which stakeholders are heavily involved as evaluation partners in all evaluation phases, as contrasted with school-based evaluation, the process by which stakeholders are involved in varying degrees at the beginning and ending phases of evaluation (Brandon, 1998). He indicates that stakeholder involvement throughout program development, implementation, and evaluation helped to validate the soundness or trustworthiness of the inferences drawn from the results of the FSCPP interventions. Moreover, he suggests that program participants are considered "experts" because they can help to shape and refine researchers' ideas and the feasibility of collaboratively designed interventions (Brandon, 1998). This perspective is closely aligned with the themes and features of the TD evaluation framework presented in Chapter One of this volume.

Developing and Implementing the Family, School, and Community Partnership Program

The TDSSP developed a collaborative partnership with a public high school that serves low-income students in an urban neighborhood in the northeastern United States as an implementation site for whole school reform including its FSCPP. Emphasizing family, school, and community members' school involvement and collaboration with TDSSP design team and evaluators, the FSCPP sought to improve stakeholder participants' (students, teachers, staff, family, and community members) knowledge of, attitudes toward, and participation in specific activities designed to improve students' academic achievement and social competence.

Five co-constructed interventions to improve program participants' knowledge of, attitudes toward, and participation in the FSCPP activities were developed, implemented, and evaluated (Jackson, LaPoint, Towns, and Manswell Butty, 2001). These interventions were co-constructed with school stakeholders—that is, evidenced-based strategies tailored to the specific schools' needs were collaboratively created:

• The Family Resource Center (FRC) and an open house event. The FRC, located in the school building, was designed and outfitted with literature, supplies, a computer, and other materials to institutionalize the school-family-community partnership programs and was used for receptions, meetings, and workshops. The FRC was designated for and used by family members, students, teachers, staff, and community members and had several outreach strategies, such as volunteer recruitment, workshops, and training courses. The open house event was convened to inform various groups about the school and FRC educational and cocurricular activities.

• The High School Action Team (HSAT), comprising educational stakeholders: students, teachers, staff, PTA representatives, family and community members, and TDSSP staff. Its members planned, guided, and monitored the implementation of FSCPP interventions and facilitated stakeholder involvement in educational programming and schoolwide committees.

• The Talent Development Attendance Program (TDAP), comprising HSAT members, attendance staff, volunteers, and TDSSP staff. It provided information through meetings, flyers, bulletin boards, and newsletters to students, teachers, and family and community members about the importance of attendance. The TDAP also implemented activities, such as focus groups, home telephone calls, attendance forms, and classroom celebrations, to monitor and reinforce student attendance.

• The Talent Development Student Team (TDST), comprising students, teachers, school administrators, and TDSSP staff. The team sought to facilitate student involvement and leadership development in FSCPP activities.

• The Newsletter Communication Network (NCN). Often written and reproduced on-site at the school, the NCN provided student academic support and social competence information relating to school and community activities to various people and groups, such as schedules of events, learning strategies, and community resources. The newsletter was mailed to families, taken home to families by students, distributed in the FRC and the school's main office, and distributed to community business and organizational sites.

Participants Engaged in Program Development and Implementation

The TD evaluation framework calls for early and ongoing engagement of key stakeholders. Therefore, after TDSSP staff made initial contact with the school administration, they met with the Local School Restructuring Team (LSRT), a school-based governance body consisting of a teachers' union representative, school administrators, counselors, teachers, and family and community members. This meeting was designed to obtain buy-in for the program. TDSSP staff presented information on co-constructing an evidenced-based program that would be collaboratively developed, implemented, and evaluated. LSRT members asked questions and provided comments about aspects of the proposed program—comments that were useful in all its stages. The meeting was successful: LSRT members approved and supported co-constructing the FSCPP.

Collaborating with school and community stakeholders, the TDSSP staff began to develop and implement the HSAT—the organizing or steering body for FSCPP activities. The HSAT members' selection, which was recommended by the school's administration, school volunteers, and community members, was based on several criteria, such as observed interaction with education stakeholders and ability to volunteer at or away from school. Additional HSAT members were later recruited from the FSCPP workshops, convened by the TDSSP staff, which focused on implementing and evaluating school-family-community practices.

The evaluation team conducted several individual and group meetings at the school to obtain informal and preliminary information about school stakeholders and the school, including building layout, organizational chart, school climate, and stakeholder morale. The meetings, which engaged participants, provided opportunities to solicit participants' views about program development and implementation—and subsequent evaluation. Discussions were recorded and summarized, with written summaries given to participants. This approach showed stakeholders that their views were valued in problem definition and solution. As reported by stakeholders and observed by TDSSP staff, the approach was empowering and effective in obtaining initial and ongoing participant buy-in. In these meetings, TDSSP staff observed participants to be alert, relaxed, and highly engaged when they openly shared their views about the nature of educational challenges and possible solutions.

Initially, a core group of seven stakeholders—students, teachers, staff, and family and community members—was recruited to assist with the FSCPP. These recruited stakeholders were either volunteers or were referred by administrators, staff, and teachers. The school stakeholders, including students, received a nominal stipend for their participation in the ongoing FSCPP process. In-service training workshops on evidence-based family, school, and community partnerships practices were initiated with the group during the summer prior to implementing the interventions. These sessions were conducted at CRESPAR facilities at Howard University and Johns Hopkins University, as well as at the participants' school site. Although evidenced-based practices were the focus, participants were encouraged to tailor practices to meet the school's specific needs. On-site FSCPP school coordinators and chairpersons, elected by HSAT members, volunteered to organize and coordinate FSCPP activities for their particular school site. The formative suggestions obtained from the urban school stakeholders assisted TDSSP staff with developing and evaluating a program that was more likely to meet stakeholder needs. Moreover, participants directly involved in program development and implementation also assisted in validating findings (Brandon, Lindberg, and Wang, 1993; Brandon, 1998).

Participant Engagement in Evaluation

HSAT participants—students, teachers, staff, and family and community members—became assistant evaluators to TDSSP evaluators and received initial and ongoing training in their evaluation role. This included information and skill sessions on the role and importance of program evaluation, instrument review meetings and data collection procedures, and effective ways to interact with program participants. Training sessions, including evaluation materials, were simple enough for participants who did have technical training to work with TDSSP evaluators.

After the training sessions, the assistant evaluators were involved in TD program evaluation that illustrated adherence to the TD evaluation strategies—of engaging stakeholders, co-construction, responsiveness, triangulation, and cultural and context relevance. First, HSAT members assisted evaluators in developing evidenced-based program goals and objectives, and therefore program outcomes. Again, HSAT members, like other school stakeholder groups, were engaged in small working groups—listening intently and openly sharing their views on educational problems and possible solutions. In the second strategy, HSAT members reviewed instruments by assisting evaluators in developing, selecting, or refining items or questions for surveys, focus groups, and interviews. Before surveys were administered to participants, they were piloted with HSAT members. Here, TD evaluators were concerned that the content of information was contextually and culturally responsive to participants' experiences in interventions. Participants provided evaluators with important feedback about the clarity and suitability of the survey and interview items and focus group questions.

In the third strategy, HSAT members provided feedback to evaluators on program implementation in formative evaluations for immediate changes in program development or implementation. This feedback to TD evaluators showed the symbiotic relationship between evaluators and implementers. Implementers could then initiate any needed changes in the program that could have a positive impact on subsequent program evaluation. HSAT members were trained and encouraged to use the participant-observation strategy to observe and record data on school-related events immediately after the activities occurred. Evaluators analyzed their observation notes to learn about the nature of participants' attitudes and behaviors within the context of HSAT's goals, objectives, and desired outcomes. Inductive observation approaches were used so that evaluators would remain open to all possibilities of refining the HSAT's interventions and allowing the data collected to inform and guide implementers and evaluators better.

HSAT also routinely assisted evaluators in reviewing written data such as students' school attendance logs and the logs that recorded student, family, and community member attendance at school events. HSAT members attended school activities and events to ensure that stakeholders signed an attendance log on entering the school building. Collecting these data allowed HSAT members to play an essential role in the evaluation process by offering insightful comments, suggestions, and recommendations for improving program evaluation strategies. Finally, HSAT members were trained to use informal interviews with program participants. The interviews provided opportunities for participants to give feedback about the functioning of the HSAT and its impact on school-related activities and events. Also, the interviews provided opportunities to validate the consistency of HSAT members' reports—what they said, how they said it, and to whom they said it.

A fourth evaluation strategy engaged HSAT members to distribute and collect surveys from stakeholder participants—students and family and community members. This strategy was a particularly meaningful data collection strategy for participants who did not return surveys by the deadlines. HSAT members had similar backgrounds to participants and could foster identification with participants—minimizing or eliminating any negative feelings about unreturned surveys while collecting the needed surveys.

Evaluation of the implementation process was ongoing throughout the academic year. HSAT members assisted evaluators by participating in quarterly focus groups conducted with participants. Upon completing the evaluation, evaluators conducted focus groups to examine results and challenges of implementing the FSCPP. Measurable differences from pretest to posttest were found among participants on variables relating to participant knowledge, attitudes, and behavior relating to the FSCPP.

These results, as well as qualitative data, showed that the FSCPP increased the knowledge and improved the attitudes toward and involvement of students, teachers and staff, and family members in high school students' education (Jackson, LaPoint, Towns, and Manswell Butty, 2001) as well as with similar interventions in a middle school (Jackson, Wallace, and LaPoint, 2003).

Several program development and implementation strategies were used to facilitate participant involvement in the FSCPP evaluation:

• Racial, ethnic, gender, age, and social class cultural similarity or familiarity between FSCPP participants and TDSSP evaluators. For example, there were efforts to match TDSSP staff and participant characteristics along the cited dimensions. Also, TDSSP staff had several consistent years of prior experience in working with low-income black participants in research, policy, program, and advocacy activities related to health, human services, and criminal justice settings as well as educational settings.

• Initial and continued rapport building and buy-in strategies to prevent and minimize insider-outsider status between FSCPP participants and TDSSP staff implementers and evaluators. For example, one strategy was to have TDSSP staff dress in business-casual attire and minimize academic jargon in discussions with participants—without talking down to participants. As a result of these strategies, staff members' interaction with participants appeared to empower participants, who generally are unaccustomed to such experiences with schools and other institutions, as evidenced by their reports, consistent punctuality and attendance, and active participation in program evaluation activities.

• Collaborative engagement of program staff in program activities over time. Although each individual grouping had prescribed roles and responsibilities—as program developers, implementers, and evaluators— some staff members had multiple roles. While these multiple roles occurred in some cases because of staff funding issues, having program evaluators in the dual roles of program developers and evaluators was an asset. For example, evaluators could use their skills to guide the fidelity of program development and implementation so that there could be more effective outcomes and evaluation. That is, evaluators could guide the development of tight programs and activities, with specific measurable objectives and outcomes. This is an important consideration in conducting school improvement interventions in urban schools serving low-income students for the reasons discussed in various chapters of this volume. Two prominent reasons are that many low-performing schools are in an ever-changing, even crisis-oriented context, and school administrators, teachers, and staff may want school improvement teams to perform services unrelated to the agreed-on co-constructed, evidenced-based school improvement agenda (for example, substitute or nonacademic resource teachers).

Implications and Conclusions: Lessons Learned

The evaluation strategies and issues presented in this chapter show how the TD evaluation approach to program evaluation may be of broad interest to the evaluation community. Some strategies may or may not be new or innovative to evaluators, who may have used some of these procedures in evaluation or as novel extensions of previous work in the evaluation field.

Many lessons can be learned from these strategies used for school improvements in program development, implementation and, ultimately, evaluation. First, evaluators should recognize that responsive program activities can be significant when participants are low-income persons of color who are generally disenfranchised from both evaluation and service delivery systems that may be developed to meet their needs. Responsive evaluation, such as approaches used in the FSCPP and espoused by the TD evaluation framework, involves engaging participants in proactive, empowering ways such as participants being recruited, trained, and used as assistant evaluators. Two other strategies to reduce the social distance between evaluators and program participants were described: casual business dress and reduced technical jargon in language.

While TD evaluation activities built on several similarities between evaluators and program participants (race/ethnicity, experiences with cultural group, and personal family background), this match may not always be possible given the realities of students in training and professionals employed as evaluators. Therefore, there is a need for future and current evaluators to obtain certain types of experiences, respectively, in training and professional development programs. For example, training programs and professional development programs should have curricula (case studies, reference materials, and expert speakers both live and on-line) that include issues described in this volume, such as enhancing cultural relevance, engaging marginalized groups in the evaluation process, and triangulating perspectives.

In the third area, the complex and dynamic nature of urban schools and communities presented challenges in the program evaluation as well as in program development and implementation: (1) differing, competing, and ever-changing school- and district-level agendas during and even after co-constructed partnership agreements; (2) frequent and unpredictable personnel changes in school and district level leadership; and (3) participants' prior negative experiences in varying school and other intervention programs in development, implementation, and evaluation stages. These challenges can occur in action research especially when conducting evaluations of newly developed and existing service delivery systems in institutions serving low-income minority groups of color. Evaluators, with other staff developers and implementers, must recognize such potential challenges in the program development and implementation stages, so that strategies can be implemented to prevent or reduce problems in the evaluation stage.

One strategy could be for staff to know as far in advance as possible which intervention sites might have more challenges than others in completing program development, implementation, and evaluation. This suggests doing investigative homework about the intervention sites and perhaps opting for the most feasible site. A second strategy is to develop high-quality relationships with several entities, such as with administrators, especially at the school level, with teachers and staff, including organizational representatives, like the LSRT described earlier, and with community members who may be able to leverage influence within and external to schools and other community-based institutions. A third strategy could be to develop feasible action plans and adhering to guidelines. A fourth strategy is to select and reward participants who are high implementers of program objectives while treating all participants with integrity. These same high implementers can be tapped to collaborate with evaluators as assistant program evaluators or critical friends in similar settings.

Fourth, contextually and culturally responsive evaluation strategies are consistent with the paradigm shift that is being recognized in research, policy, and programs, including advocacy where an asset-based approach instead of a deficit approach is being used with child and adult program participants (Boykin, 2000; Delpit, 2003; Denby, 1996; Hill, 1997). When an asset-based approach as opposed to a deficit-oriented approach is used, a more balanced view of populations can emerge. In using an asset- or strengths-based approach, more effective programs can be designed to promote human development, especially the development of culturally diverse, marginalized populations. Responsive evaluation also focuses on participants' assets, where these characteristics can be identified and used as valuable feedback in program development and implementation. This is an important issue when working with low-income groups of color who are often disenfranchised. All of these strategies have implications for how program action plans, including staffing, are budgeted and administered.

Although this chapter focused on the evaluation of a school-based intervention, the evaluation community can use lessons learned from this approach to evaluate programs in service delivery systems in health, human services, social welfare, and criminal justice. This is especially relevant in conducting programs with low-income groups of color whose voices are often omitted, minimized, or viewed negatively. Evaluators implementing school-based evaluation programs may wish to consider adopting some of the strategies described in this chapter. These methods helped to ensure the infusion of stakeholders' expertise in several evaluation areas: survey items, focus group items, and informal interviews. Moreover, ongoing stakeholders' participation in program evaluation can elevate evaluators' confidence of the validity of the conclusions they draw from programs developed, implemented, and evaluated. Given the demand for high-quality programs and services in educational and other settings, there is a need for evaluations that are both responsive to program participants and accountable to funding organizations. The evaluation strategies discussed in this chapter can contribute to program development, implementation, and evaluation fidelity.

References

Argyris, C., and Schön, D. A. "Participatory Action Research and Action Research Science Compared: A Commentary." In W. F. Whyte (ed.), *Participatory Action Research.* Thousand Oaks, Calif.: Sage, 1991.

Berger, E. H. *Parents as Partners in Education: Families and Schools Working Together.* Upper Saddle River, N.J.: Prentice Hall, 2003.

Boykin, A. W. "The Talent Development Model of Schooling: Placing Students at Promise for Academic Success." *Journal of Education for Students Placed at Risk,* 2000, *5*(1/2), 3–25.

Brandon, P. R. "Stakeholder Participation for the Purpose of Helping Ensure Evaluation Validity: Bridging the Gap Between Collaborative and Non-Collaborative Evaluation. *American Journal of Evaluation,* 1998, *19*(3), 325–337.

Brandon, P. R., Lindberg, M. A., and Wang, Z. "Involving Program Beneficiaries in the Early Stages of Evaluation: Issues of Consequential Validity and Influence." *Educational Evaluation and Policy Analysis,* 1993, *15,* 420–428.

Brotherton, P. "Beacons of Hope: SECME Inc. Partners with Minority-Serving Institutions to Create Alternative High Schools to Increase High School, College Completion Rates." *Black Issues in Higher Education,* 2003, *20*(8), 20–23.

Carroll, G., LaPoint, V., and Tyler, K. "Co-Construction: A Facilitator for School Reform in School, Community, and University Partnerships." *Journal of Negro Education,* 2001, *70*(1/2), 38–58.

Cousins, J. B., and Earl, L. M. (eds.). *Participatory Evaluation in Education: Studies in Evaluation Use and Organizational Learning.* Bristol, Pa.: Falmer, 1995.

Delpit, L. "Educators as 'Seed People' Growing a New Future." *Educational Researcher,* 2003, *7*(22), 14–21.

Denby, R. W. "Resiliency and the African American Family: A Model of Family Preservation." In S. L. Logan (ed.), *The Black Family: Strengths, Self-Help, and Positive Change.* Boulder, Colo.: Westview, 1996.

Duffy, F., and Dale, J. *Creating Successful School Systems: Voices from the University, the Field, and the Community.* Norwalk, Conn.: Christopher-Gordon, 2001.

Education Trust. "A New Core Curriculum for All: Aiming High for Other People's Children." *Thinking K–16,* 2003, *1*(7), 32 pages (special issue).

Epstein, J. L. *School, Family, and Community Partnerships: Preparing Educators and Improving Schools.* Boulder, Colo.: Westview, 2001.

Epstein, J. L. *School, Family, and Community Partnerships: Your Handbook for Action.* New York: Corwin, 2002.

Hill, R. *The Strengths of African American Families: Twenty-Five Years Later.* Lanham, Md.: University Press of America, 1997.

Jackson, H. L., LaPoint, V., Towns, D. P., and Manswell Butty, J. "Creating a Family Resource Center in the Context of a Talent Development High School." *Journal of Negro Education,* 2001, *70*(1/2), 96–113.

Jackson, H. L., Wallace, M., and LaPoint, V. "Implementation of the Talent Development Family-School-Community Partnership Component at a Middle School of Students Placed at Risk." Unpublished manuscript, 2003.

Maurrasse, D. J. *Beyond the Campus: How Colleges and Universities Form Partnerships with Their Communities.* New York: Routledge, 2001.

Posavac, E. J., and Carey, R. G. *Program Evaluation: Methods and Case Studies.* (6th ed.) Upper Saddle River, N.J.: Prentice Hall, 2003.

Sanders, M. G. *Schools, Families, and Communities: Partnerships for Success.* Reston, Va.: National Association of Secondary School Principals, 2001.

Torres, R. T., Preskill, H. S., and Piontek, M. E. *Evaluation Strategies for Communication and Reporting: Enhancing Learning in Organizations.* Thousand Oaks, Calif.: Sage, 1996.

Wright, K., and Stegelin, D. A. *Building School and Community Partnerships Through Parent Involvement.* Upper Saddle River, N.J.: Merrill Prentice Hall, 2003.

VELMA LAPOINT is principal investigator of the Talent Development Secondary School Project at the Howard University Center for Research on the Education of Students Placed At Risk and associate professor, Department of Human Development and Psychoeducational Studies, School of Education, Howard University.

HENRY L. JACKSON is project director of the Family, School, and Community Partnership Program of the Talent Development Secondary School Project at the Howard University Center for Research on the Education of Students Placed At Risk.

3

This chapter discusses the evaluation of an urban school-to-career intervention program using a culturally responsive approach, highlighting the successes and challenges experienced during the design and implementation of the study.

A Culturally Responsive Evaluation Approach Applied to the Talent Development School-to-Career Intervention Program

Jo-Anne L. Manswell Butty, Malva Daniel Reid, Velma LaPoint

Program evaluation has long been used to reveal program characteristics, merits, and challenges. While providing information about program effectiveness, evaluations can also ensure understanding of program outcomes, efficiency, and quality. Furthermore, evaluations can analyze and examine a program's political and social environment as well as appraise the achievement of its goals, objectives, impact, and costs (Posavac and Carey, 2003). Another important factor in conducting evaluations is their cultural responsiveness. Consideration of this factor seems quite obvious, but in our opinion remains uncommon.

In the United States, numerous programs in various settings are having an effect on individuals of all types. Within the past three decades, there have been shifts to identify and meet program needs of these diverse populations and to make evaluations more inclusive of all cultures. This shift has helped in documenting program processes, effectiveness, and outcomes, as well as providing specific benefits to projects and their stakeholders.

The work reported herein was supported by grant(s) from the Institute of Education Sciences (IES) (formerly the Office of Educational Research and Improvement), U.S. Department of Education. The findings and opinions expressed in this chapter do not necessarily reflect the position or policies of the Institute of Education Sciences or the U.S. Department of Education.

Examples of shifts can be seen in the emergence of evaluation paradigms that include responsive evaluation (Abma and Stake, 2001; Stake, 1976, 1983), collaborative evaluation (Brandon, 1998), participatory evaluation (Cousins and Whitmore, 1998; King, 1998), feminist evaluation (Hood and Cassaro, 2002), mixed-method evaluation (McConney, Rudd, and Ayres, 2002), inclusive evaluation (Mertens, 1999, 2003), and empowerment evaluation (Fetterman, 2003). These shifts are important to ensure evaluation validity in all its forms (methodological, cultural, interpersonal, and consequential), and they can ultimately lead to increased advocacy, social betterment, and justice (Kirkhart, 1995; Greene, 2000; Mark and Henry, 2002).

Within the domain of education, of particular interest today are evaluations of programs situated in different settings, including urban settings. For these settings, one can ask questions such as: How useful and valid are identified program outcomes? How can staff design evaluations to ensure all stakeholders feel empowered and part of the evaluation process? How can evaluators include the context and culture of program participants during the evaluation process? Since traditional evaluation models cannot easily answer these questions, evaluation research needs to be extended to focus on the range of evidence available through other nontraditional evaluation models.

This chapter explores some of the successes and challenges encountered in evaluating a Howard University Center for Research on the Education of Students Placed At Risk (CRESPAR) urban school-to-career intervention program using a culturally responsive approach.

Culturally Responsive Evaluations

Little research has been conducted to examine how newer evaluation paradigms, such as culturally responsive evaluation, have defined, assessed, and interpreted program outcomes and impact in urban schools. This is important because evaluators in urban settings are faced with issues of inclusion and exclusion, cultural diversity, and responsiveness. Thomas (Chapter One, this volume) and others (for example, Frierson, Hood, and Hughes, 2002) describe an evaluation as culturally responsive if it fully takes into account the culture of the program being evaluated. They add that this type of evaluation seeks to fully describe and explain the context of the program being evaluated. In culturally responsive evaluations, evaluators honor the cultural context in which an evaluation takes place by bringing needed shared life experiences and understandings to the evaluation task at hand.

Three key terms are infused in this definition of culturally responsive evaluation: *context, culture,* and *responsive evaluation.* The context of an evaluation, as defined by Thomas (Chapter One, this volume), is the combination of factors accompanying the implementation and evaluation of a project that might influence its results, including geographical location, timing, political and social climate, economic conditions, and other things going on at the same time. In other words, it includes the totality of the environment in which a project takes place. The word *culture* is defined as the shared values, traditions, norms, customs, arts, history, folklore, and institutions of a group of people. In this case, culture shapes how people see their world and structure their community and other aspects of their lives. Finally, the term *responsive evaluation* is described as an evaluation that responds to audience requirements for information and takes into account the different value perspectives held by stakeholders in reporting a program's successes and failures. In school-based programs, the audience could be program funders or school administrators. Stakeholders at these sites may involve administrators, teachers and other school staff, students, and family and community members. From a responsive evaluation perspective, stakeholders' involvement in the program evaluation is important because these individuals have a wealth of knowledge to share.

In reviewing the culturally responsive debate, Frierson, Hood, and Hughes (2002) indicate that not everyone agrees that culturally responsive evaluation is a good idea. They assert two frequently stated arguments against using this strategy in educational evaluations: the claim that evaluations should be culture free and that while an evaluation should take into account the culture and values of a project or program it is examining, it should not be responsive to them. For the former claim, Frierson, Hood, and Hughes argue that there are no culture-free evaluations, educational tests, or societal laws. In other words, values are reflected in social activities, whether they are educational, governmental, or legal. The responsibility of educational evaluators is to recognize their own personal cultural preferences and to make a conscious effort to restrict any undue influence they might have on the work.

For the second claim, Frierson, Hood, and Hughes argue that it is important not only to recognize and describe the cultural context of a program, it is also critical to adopt evaluation strategies that are consonant with and thereby respond to the cultural context under examination. This is partly because of the changing American demographics whereby society is becoming racially, ethnically, and linguistically diverse, as well as recognition of the role that fullness or completeness of description plays in a comprehensive evaluation process. At CRESPAR, we argue that it is important for program designers, implementers, and evaluators to understand the cultural context in which programs operate. Under this premise, we provide a case example of how we evaluated a Talent Development urban school intervention using a culturally responsive approach. In this chapter, the emphasis is placed on implementing a culturally responsive evaluation approach and not the findings of the evaluation.

Introduction to the Intervention

CRESPAR established a formal partnership with several public schools in a northeastern metropolitan area. One project operating under CRESPAR is the Talent Development Secondary School Project (SSP), which, like all other CRESPAR projects, subscribes to the Talent Development Model of

School Reform (Boykin, 2000). The Talent Development School-to-Career Transitions Intervention is one of four interventions of the SSP.

The School-to-Career Transitions intervention took place at a junior high school (grades 7 to 9) located in an urban district in the northeastern part of the United States. The population at the junior high school is approximately three hundred students. The twenty-nine staff members represent varied national origins and years of teaching experience. At this school, about 78 percent of the students are eligible to receive free or reduced-price lunch, about one-third are classified as special education students, and over 95 percent are African American.

The major goal of the school-to-career intervention at the targeted school site was to improve the knowledge, attitudes, and practices of urban students related to school-to-career development opportunities as they make the transition from elementary to middle school, middle to high school, and high school to postsecondary options such as college, technical training, and employment through a variety of learning activities.

The project's evaluation questions addressed student perceptions of the materials used, new and relevant student learning, and ultimately how students reported they would use this learning as they move on to high school. We expected improvements in their knowledge, attitudes, and practices toward career development, exploration, and school transitioning activities. Through the administration of qualitative and quantitative assessments such as student career interests, surveys, interviews, and focus groups, we collected data to answer our evaluation questions and assess our outcomes.

The school-to-career intervention was the Ninth-Grade Career Breakfast Club, conducted with seventeen ninth-grade students after they completed their standardized examinations (Stanford Achievement Test, Ninth Edition) in April 2003. These students were scheduled to graduate from junior high school in June 2003. The month-long Breakfast Club consisted of eight one-hour sessions that took place before the start of the formal school day, from 7:45 to 8:45 A.M. It allowed students to become more aware of career-related areas by including information about their own career aspirations as indicated on the Holland Self-Directed Search Self-Assessment and other indicators; the broad spectrum of careers and occupations in demand; resources and search skills to access information about college, careers, technical training, and employment opportunities; and social skills and information needed to promote high-quality school-to-career transitions (in communication, specific vocabulary, and resumé writing, for example).

Along with interactive discussion groups and activities, student participants in the Breakfast Club also received a complimentary breakfast, an up-to-date career notebook, a certificate of participation, and a small stipend. Among the topics discussed during the meetings with students were pathways to college, entrepreneurship, completing a job application, writing a resumé, and how to handle a job interview. Along with the eight workshops, participants completed session evaluations, self-assessments, and pre- and posttests. Self- and standardized assessments and various learning activities were designed to make students aware of their own interests, talents, and assets, as well as the broad spectrum of education and training opportunities in colleges, technical institutions, and careers.

This intervention was developed in part by reviewing the literature in the area of career development and exploration for adolescents. Of particular interest was the literature pertaining to students of color. In past years, we had collected data related to career development and exploration of middle school students through surveys and focus group interviews with students, teachers, and family members. This information was synthesized with the current review of the literature. Following the literature review, TD staff collaborated with the teachers, staff, and students at this school site to co-construct school-to-career program activities, conduct needs assessments related to career areas for students, develop materials and strategies to facilitate eight workshops on relevant career topics for students, and evaluate program activities.

A Contextually Responsive Approach to Evaluating the Career Breakfast Club

Consistent with the underlying approach and themes of the TD evaluation framework, Frierson, Hood, and Hughes (2002) view eight phases of the evaluation process as critical in conducting culturally responsive evaluations:

1. Preparing for the evaluation
2. Engaging stakeholders
3. Identifying the purpose and intent of the evaluation
4. Framing the right questions
5. Selecting and adapting instrumentation
6. Collecting data
7. Analyzing the data
8. Disseminating and using the results

The following discussion examines how the evaluation of the Ninth Grade Career Breakfast Club measured up to this culturally responsive approach.

Preparing for the Evaluation. In preparing for the evaluation, TD staff held meetings with stakeholders at the school on at least four occasions to plan the intervention and evaluation. This was done in an effort to fully understand the sociocultural context of the environment in which the intervention and evaluation would take place. During these meetings, as TD staff, we not only heard what the stakeholders had to say, but sought to listen carefully to what was being said. Meetings with the school principal, counselor, and liaison allowed TD staff to review student profiles on their goals and aspirations, meet some of the students and teachers, get feedback on activities planned, and select appropriate assessments. In preparing for the evaluation, genuine collaboration was promoted in order to co-construct program and evaluation activities with stakeholders. This collaboration was manifested through sharing school documents and research findings, exchanging ideas with key stakeholders—school principal, liaison, and counselor—on issues of program and evaluation activities, and persisting in efforts to tailor the proposed intervention to the school, keeping student, family, and community factors in mind.

Engaging Stakeholders. One of the major themes of the TD evaluation framework is that of engaging stakeholders. An initial step in designing a culturally responsive evaluation is the identification of the key stakeholders, essential because these individuals play a critical role in providing sound advice from the beginning of the evaluation process (framing questions) to the end (disseminating the evaluation results). In the school-to-career intervention, we were fortunate that the school-based stakeholders were extremely supportive of our intervention and evaluation efforts. We engaged the school principal, school liaison, and school counselor. Our key point of contact was the school liaison. This individual had a background in counseling psychology; over thirty years of public school experience; expert procedural and conceptual knowledge about program development, implementation, and evaluation in urban school settings; and a genuine regard for the welfare of students at her school, all of which enhanced the stakeholder engagement process. In addition, the school principal fully supported our efforts. As a result, we were able to freely debate ideas and ask for and use suggestions to frame our evaluation questions, implement our plans, and disseminate our results in ways to enhance use by key stakeholders.

Identifying the Purpose and Intent of the Evaluation. The evaluation team ensured there was a clear understanding of the evaluation's purpose, intent, and results. Conducting both formative and summative evaluations helped to facilitate this process. The formative evaluations measured and described program operations in order to inform project staff for the purpose of making improvements as needed. TD evaluators reviewed the students' comments after each session and provided the results to the program design team. This process fostered ongoing feedback and led to improvements (formative) and learning about outcomes (summative). Using a culturally responsive approach, the project team always discussed the progress of the program after each session and made improvements to keep students' interest levels high. In other words, feedback from the students was used to fine-tune subsequent sessions to make them more valuable and enjoyable. This demonstrates one example of engaging and valuing stakeholder input in both the intervention design and evaluation process. The summative evaluations revealed whether and to what extent the intervention achieved its objectives. For the summative evaluations, as a culturally responsive team, we examined the direct effects of the program implementation on the participants and attempted to explain the results within the context of the program.

Framing the Right Questions. In culturally responsive evaluations, it is critical that the questions of significant stakeholders be heard and, where appropriate, addressed (Frierson, Hood, and Hughes, 2002). Here, the evaluation questions were carefully considered not only by the evaluator and project staff, but by other stakeholders—school principal, liaison, and counselor—as well. The framing of research and evaluation questions for the TD School-to-Career Transitions Intervention was initially formulated at the project level by the project developers, implementers, and evaluator during the stage of preparing for the evaluation. Subsequently, we constructed a data map or a matrix that visually displayed the TD intervention objectives, interventions and activities, research and evaluation questions, measures, data collection, expected outcomes, project staff responsibilities, and school staff responsibilities. This data map was then shared with the school staff for their review and feedback. In working as a team (TD intervention designers, implementer, and evaluator) to lay out the evaluation framework and share it with the school staff for their feedback, we were able to feel confident about the evaluation questions we had proposed.

Designing the Evaluation. Numerous investigators promote evaluation designs that include both a qualitative and quantitative component (Frierson, Hood, and Hughes, 2002; Greene and Caracelli, 1997; Greene, Caracelli, and Graham, 1989; Chapter Four, this volume). The TD evaluation approach promotes triangulation of conceptual and methodological perspectives. In addition, designs that incorporate data collection at multiple times provide an opportunity to examine the degree to which some aspects of the participants' behavior changed as a result of the project interventions. Furthermore, when comparison or control groups are incorporated into the pretest-posttest design, evaluators are able to determine to what extent some aspects of participants' behavior change relative to where it would have been had they not been exposed to the project intervention. For this intervention, the evaluation design incorporated both qualitative (for example, written comments, interviews) and quantitative (for example, surveys, self-assessments), as well as a pretest-posttest, design. To facilitate participation of all respondents, we paid particular attention to adapting data collection schedules. We had to spread out the administration of surveys and self-assessments since many students preferred discussions and other interactive activities rather than filling out surveys and self-assessments. Furthermore, the self-assessment was administered to the study group as well as to all other ninth-grade students attending the school, creating a comparison group to measure the career self-assessment dimension of the study. The data obtained were combined with other qualitative and quantitative data already collected to examine trends among gender and age.

Selecting and Adapting Instrumentation. Clearly, the selection of appropriate measurements is a critical area of concern when doing culturally responsive evaluations. At the most basic level, instruments should be identified, developed, or adapted to capture the kinds and types of information needed to answer the evaluation questions (Frierson, Hood, and Hughes, 2002). Often, instruments used on populations of color have been normed on majority populations, calling into question the validity of inferences drawn. This was the case for one of our instruments. We sought to counter this by collecting other data about the participants to be added to the data obtained from the measure. Also, other instruments used to evaluate program participants were reviewed and selected for use based on the extent to which they were culturally sensitive by means of their form, language, and content.

Collecting Data. Culturally responsive evaluations make substantial use of qualitative evaluation data collection techniques. In these instances, there must be recognition of self-as-instrument, or acknowledging that the person collecting the data is also, essentially, an instrument (Frierson, Hood, and Hughes, 2002). Therefore, an instrument (or individual) that is an improper measure provides invalid data. In other words, if those who are collecting and recording the data are not attuned to the cultural context in which the program is situated, the collected data could be invalid. As individuals with a shared racial background with the stakeholders, TD project team members went into the urban school context with an increased level of sensitivity and awareness to the plight and lived experiences of the various stakeholder groups. In collecting qualitative data for the school-to-career intervention, as when conducting one-on-one and group interviews, the evaluator was sensitive to the context and culture of the participants. Gathering and becoming familiar with information on the context of the school before the intervention took place enhanced the evaluator's contextual sensitivity. Also, the evaluator's participation in multiple meetings with key stakeholder groups, as well as participation in and observation of other school-related functions, provided additional knowledge not gleaned from written documents.

Analyzing the Data. Determining the accurate meaning of what has been observed is central in culturally responsive evaluation. This can be accomplished by thoroughly knowing the language nuances of the group's culture being studied and by disaggregating the collected data, beyond the analysis of whole group data, in order to derive valid meaning from the findings. Input was derived from various school stakeholders on how best to analyze and interpret the data in ways that provided meaning in their particular context. On a most basic level, the findings for this intervention were disaggregated by gender and age to get a breakdown of career attitudes and beliefs for African American male and female participants at different ages and developmental stages. Although students were in the ninth grade, their ages ranged from fourteen to sixteen.

Disseminating and Using the Results. Audiences should view the evaluation results as not only useful but truthful as well. Culturally responsive evaluations can increase the likelihood that the results will be perceived as useful and, indeed, used. For this school-to-career intervention, along with giving students feedback about their evaluation findings in a student-friendly manner, findings were disseminated to the school principal, liaison, and counselor. In addition to summarizing the results, the findings highlighted successes, challenges, and other limitations of the program. A report was also sent to funders and other project staff with a stake or interest in the project.

Implications and Conclusions

Three of the key themes in the TD evaluation framework are engaging stakeholders, cultural and contextual relevance, and triangulation. Evaluators working within a culturally responsive approach are challenged to find appropriate ways to implement this approach. Many evaluators and practitioners who operate within a limited evaluation framework may believe there is only one way to do evaluations, may not ask and examine important questions, may come up short when attempting to evaluate complex systems, and may lose sight of the fact that all evaluation work is political and value laden (W. K. Kellogg Foundation, 1998). From the perspective of those who work with underserved populations, this approach may reflect a limited view that hinders the ability to understand the richness and complexity of programs and their participants. As a result, implications for culturally responsive evaluators include incorporating a team approach (including key stakeholders, program developers, specialists, implementers, and evaluators) and working collaboratively toward implementing and evaluating interventions; understanding and being responsive to aspects of the culture and context at all times during the evaluation process; being flexible enough to combine different evaluation approaches for different situations; and sharing evaluation successes (and failures). Our TD efforts respected the cultural context of the intervention and evaluation and allowed for greater collaboration among stakeholders and project staff, higher engagement among program participants, and evaluation findings that were useful and valid. This approach led to an intervention and evaluation that benefited stakeholders and participants, as evidenced by student and staff evaluations and positive student outcomes.

Clearly, successes and challenges arose when we were evaluating this intervention from a culturally responsive approach. Perhaps most important, conducting this type of evaluation was labor intensive, especially with a limited number of project staff. This limitation meant that TD staff had to perform multiple roles to meet the needs of the school and its students, staff, and families. Project staff sometimes switched roles from developer to evaluator to curriculum specialist. We believe that it was beneficial that the evaluator was involved in all aspects of program planning and implementation. The full cooperation and support received from the school staff and the interest and concern of the project staff enabled the intervention to work.

The use of a culturally responsive program evaluation approach in urban schools provides guidelines for evaluators to achieve a fuller understanding of how and why projects and programs work. This approach allows them to get inside a project and understand roles, responsibilities, structure, history, and goals. Subsequently, using this information to implement an evaluation process that is culturally responsive to examining the evaluation questions and dealing with the effects of paradigms, politics, and values allows for a better understanding of the problem. The combination of a greater sensitivity to stakeholder needs and a deeper respect for the importance of culture and context of the program are crucial steps toward improvement in program evaluations.

References

Abma, T. A., and Stake, R. E. "Stake's Responsive Evaluation: Core Ideas and Evolution." In J. S. Greene and T. A. Abma (eds.), *Responsive Evaluation.* New Directions for Evaluation, no. 92. San Francisco: Jossey-Bass, 2001.

Boykin, A. W. "The Talent Development Model of Schooling. Placing Students at Promise for Academic Success." *Journal of Education for Students Placed at Risk,* 2000, 5(1/2), 3–25.

Brandon, P. R. "Stakeholder Participation for the Purpose of Helping Ensure Evaluation Validity: Bridging the Gap Between Collaborative and Non-Collaborative Evaluations." *American Journal of Evaluation,* 1998, *19*(3), 325–337.

Cousins, J. B., and Whitmore, E. "Framing Participatory Evaluation." In E. Whitmore (ed.), *Understanding and Practicing Participatory Evaluation.* New Directions For Evaluation, no. 80. San Francisco: Jossey-Bass, 1998.

Fetterman, D. "Empowerment Evaluation Strikes a Responsive Chord." In S. I. Donaldson and M. Scriven (eds.), *Evaluating Social Programs and Problems: Visions for the New Millennium.* Mahwah, N.J.: Erlbaum, 2003.

Frierson, H. T., Hood, S., and Hughes, G. B. "Strategies That Address Culturally Responsive Evaluations." In J. Frechtling (ed.), *The 2002 User-Friendly Handbook for Project Evaluation.* Arlington, Va.: National Science Foundation, 2002.

Greene, J. C. "Challenges in Practicing Deliberative Democratic Evaluation." In K. E. Ryan and L. DeStefano (eds.), *Evaluation as a Democratic Process: Promoting Inclusion, Dialogue, and Deliberation.* New Directions for Evaluation, no. 85. San Francisco: Jossey-Bass, 2000.

Greene, J. C., and Caracelli, V. J. (eds.). *Advances in Mixed-Method Evaluation: The Challenges and Benefits of Integrating Diverse Paradigms.* New Directions for Program Evaluation, no. 74, San Francisco: Jossey-Bass, 1997.

Greene, J. C., Caracelli, V. J., and Graham, W. F. "Toward a Conceptual Framework for Mixed-Method Evaluation Designs." *Educational Evaluation and Policy Analysis,* 1989, 11, 255–274.

Hood, D., and Cassaro, D. A. "Feminist Evaluation and the Inclusion of Difference." In D. Seigart and S. Brisolara (eds.), *Feminist Evaluation Exploration and Experiences.* New Directions for Evaluation, no. 96. San Francisco: Jossey-Bass, 2002.

King, J. A. "Making Sense of Participatory Evaluation Practice." In E. Whitmore (ed.), *Understanding and Practicing Participatory Evaluation.* New Directions for Evaluation, no. 80. San Francisco: Jossey-Bass, 1998.

Kirkhart, K. E. "Seeking Multicultural Validity: A Postcard from the Road." *Evaluation Practice*, 1995, *16*, 1–12.

Mark, M. M., and Henry, G. T. "Influencing Attitudes and Actions: The Mechanisms and Outcomes of Evaluation Influence." Paper presented at the European Evaluation Association Meeting, Seville, Spain, 2002.

McConney, A., Rudd, A., and Ayres, R. "Getting to the Bottom Line: Synthesizing Findings Within Mixed-Method Program Evaluations." *American Journal of Evaluation*, 2002, *23*(2) 121–140.

Mertens, D. M. "Inclusive Evaluation: Implications for Transformative Theory for Evaluation." *American Journal of Evaluation*, 1999, *20*(1), 1–14.

Mertens, D. M. "The Inclusive View of Evaluation: Visions for the New Millennium." In S. I. Donaldson and M. Scriven (eds.), *Evaluating Social Programs and Problems: Visions for the New Millennium*. Mahwah, N.J.: Erlbaum, 2003.

Prosavac, E. J., and Carey, R. G. *Program Evaluation: Methods and Case Studies*. (6th ed.) Upper Saddle River, N.J.: Prentice Hall, 2003.

Stake, R. E. "A Theoretical Statement of Responsive Evaluation." *Studies in Educational Evaluation*, 1976, *2*(1), 19–22.

Stake, R. E. "Responsive Evaluation." In T. Husen and T. N. Postlewaite (eds.), *International Encyclopedia of Education: Research and Studies*. New York: Pergamon Press, 1983.

W. K. Kellogg Foundation. *W. K. Kellogg Foundation Evaluation Handbook*. Battle Creek, Mich.: W. K. Kellogg Foundation, 1998.

Jo-Anne L. Manswell Butty is project director for research and evaluation for the Secondary School Project at the Center for Research on the Education of Students Placed At Risk, Howard University, Washington, D.C.

Malva Daniel Reid is a consultant to the School-to-Career Intervention, Secondary School Project at the Center for Research on the Education of Students Placed At Risk, Howard University, Washington, D.C.

Velma LaPoint is principal investigator of the Talent Development Secondary School Project at the Howard University Center for Research on the Education of Students Placed At Risk and associate professor, Department of Human Development and Psychoeducational Studies, School of Education, Howard University, Washington, D.C.

This chapter illustrates how triangulating evaluation methodologies allow for stakeholder involvement and revealed contexts that a narrower approach might fail to illuminate.

Successes and Challenges in Triangulating Methodologies in Evaluations of Exemplary Urban Schools

Donna Penn Towns, Zewelanji Serpell

The Exemplary Schools study at Howard University's Center for Research on the Education of Students Placed At Risk (CRESPAR) was designed to aid the program in its goal toward developing and implementing a reform model that "overdetermines" success for all students. The Talent Development (TD) principle of "overdetermination of success" argues that across the full spectrum of the schooling enterprise, we must implement multiple activities, any one of which, based on documented, research-based evidence, can lead to enhanced outcomes by itself (Boykin, 2000). In preparation for designing the Exemplary Schools project, a thorough review of the effective school reform literature (for example, Cuban, 1983; Duignan, 1986; Edmonds, 1979; Mace-Matluck, 1987; Sammons and others, 1995; Stedman, 1987; Townsend, 1993; Wimpelberg, Teddlie, and Stringfield, 1987; Witte and Walsh, 1990) was undertaken.

The Exemplary Schools study aim was not only to identify practices in urban schools that were already demonstrating success, but also to inform the development of an evaluation instrument that honored the TD principles

The work reported herein was supported by grant(s) from the Institute of Education Sciences (IES) (formerly the Office of Educational Research and Improvement), U.S. Department of Education. The findings and opinions expressed in this chapter do not necessarily reflect the position or policies of the Institute of Education Sciences or the U.S. Department of Education.

of cultural sensitivity and co-construction. This chapter demonstrates how the triangulating evaluation methodologies facilitated stakeholder involvement and revealed contexts that a narrower approach might have failed to illuminate, and it highlights how triangulation can be used to create a culturally responsive evaluation process. In our study, this process significantly enhanced our ability to interpret quantitative data derived from a questionnaire, often providing evidence that refuted inferences initially drawn, and contributing to a richer understanding of the factors that make the schools we sampled exemplary. The hope is that in describing the application of the TD principles and the interdisciplinary analysis of seemingly contradictory findings, we can provide important information to others engaged in the school evaluation process.

From the outset, we sought to engage multiple stakeholders in the development and evaluation stages of this study on exemplary urban schools. The insights gained from observing and listening to stakeholders were invaluable. We became aware that an evaluation of success could not be based on a single criterion or an a priori set of criteria; rather, mutually exclusive criteria were possible and had to be viewed in terms of the overall cultural milieu of the context. For example, in our discussion with school principals, it became clear that leadership in successful urban schools can take many different forms: some principals were new to their schools, while others had been at their school site for more than twenty years; some were authoritarian and others co-constructive in approach; some principals imposed external disciplinary measures, yet others fostered the development of self-discipline. Although a similar degree of variation in teachers' attitudes and responses was observed across schools, the one commonality evident at all school sites was student engagement. It was therefore necessary for our evaluation process to take into special account the dynamics of student-adult relationships.

From the study's inception and consistent with the TD evaluation framework (discussed in Chapter One, this volume), we recognized the importance of conceptualizing evaluation in terms of both quantitative and qualitative measures. However, we were not totally aware until data analysis of the significance of reconciling disparities in findings yielded by the two sets of measures and the depth that doing so could bring to our study.

The Process

In identifying an appropriate sample for our study, we looked for urban schools where minority students were performing at or above grade level on standardized tests for two or more years. This was simply the starting point, because from a TD perspective, judging success using only results from standardized tests is insufficient. As discussed by other CRESPAR evaluators (Boykin, 2000; Jagers and Carrol, 2002), school effectiveness is not determined solely by student achievement on standardized tests, but encompasses a broader range of intended student outcomes, including:

- Enhanced intellectual achievement, of which test scores are only a part
- High levels of academic motivation
- Improved academic task engagement
- Increased social-emotional competence
- More positive school attendance behaviors
- Heightened school, community, and cultural identification

A number of organizational qualities have also been identified as characteristics of schools that successfully serve low-income, urban African American students (Cole-Henderson, 2000). The factors that contribute to fostering a broader range of positive outcomes, as delineated above, in students are not often articulated in the literature and are rarely included or discussed in reports as student outcomes. It was therefore important to us that our evaluation process include these elements and demonstrate how they factor into educational success for high-poverty urban African American students.

Evaluation Methods

A key theme in the TD evaluation framework is triangulation, or the use of mixed methods. Consistent with this perspective, we decided from the beginning that both quantitative and qualitative methods would be used to explore the factors that enable African American students in some high-poverty urban schools to obtain high test scores while nationally their counterparts are failing. The benefits of triangulation in providing both breadth and depth to any study have been well documented (Janesick, 1994; Greene, Caracelli, and Graham, 1989; Flick, 1992). In the current climate, we no longer have to justify the use of qualitative research methods as a legitimate method of arriving at certain kinds of truth, but we are still confronted with the challenge of establishing the reliability and reproducibility of findings. Triangulation comes closest to satisfying both the positivist and the phenomenological traditions. Just as three dimensions give an in-depth perspective to the eye, triangulation allows for a deeper, multifaceted view of the picture under study.

As a strategy of inquiry, triangulation can mean one or more of several things. Janesick (1994) has identified five types of triangulation:

- Data triangulation—the use of a variety of data sources
- Investigator triangulation—the use of several different evaluators
- Theory triangulation—the use of multiple perspectives to interpret a single set of data
- Methodological triangulation—the use of multiple methods to study a single problem
- Interdisciplinary triangulation—bringing theory and practice from different disciplines to bear on the problem

All of these strategies figured to some extent in our study and are consistent with the theme of triangulation inherent in the TD evaluation framework. Important to note is that while triangulation technically refers to tripartite action, the term is often used when more than three different approaches are used (Janesick, 1994). This is not problematic. Other evaluators consider the term *triangulation* simply a metaphor for obtaining a multidimensional picture of phenomena under study. At CRESPAR, we sometimes refer to our method as polyangulation.

The Exemplary Schools project encompassed many levels of triangulation. We used multiple sources of data, drawing on information provided by school administrators, support staff, teachers, students, and parents. We had methodological triangulation, using quantitative and qualitative strategies, including paper-and-pencil questionnaires, observations, and interviews. We had investigator triangulation, with a project team consisting of a statistician, sociologist, educator, psychologist, and anthropologist. We had interdisciplinary triangulation, examining the data from the perspectives of investigators representing various disciplines who brought their unique theoretical perspectives to bear on issues.

The first step in our study was to obtain from across the nation a broad database of schools and their characteristics. The second and third steps were identifying and conducting in-depth, in-the-field studies of a select set of schools that met preestablished exemplary urban school criteria. There were multiple sources for the identification and nomination of schools that met our success criteria. Contacts were made with the following:

- Evaluators engaged in effective schools research
- Major educational organizations
- The National Council of Great City Schools
- The federal Office of Educational Research and Improvement Entities
- Designers and implementers of various national reform models

These contacts yielded sixty-two schools as potential participants in our study.

All of the schools served a predominantly low-income African American student population, and at least 50 percent of their student body scored at or above grade level on a state or locally mandated test for at least two years prior to the study's initiation. The vast majority of nominated schools were elementary schools (there were fifty-one of these), but the sample also included one elementary–middle school, three middle schools, and seven high schools.

Quantitative Phase. Questionnaires were sent to the principals of the nominated schools. Twenty-nine questionnaires were completed, representing a 47 percent return rate for the total sample. As an incentive to complete the questionnaire and as compensation for their time, principals were given a monetary stipend. Of the twenty-nine schools that returned questionnaires, seventeen were eliminated because the schools were either magnets or charter schools, or their test scores were lower than had been previously reported by the nominating entity.

The mailed, self-administered questionnaire contained sections on parental involvement, effective practices, school mission, expectations, school climate, environment, opportunity to learn, the principal's instructional leadership, staff development, assessment, teacher behavior, curricula, and other school qualities. The questionnaire consisted of forty-eight questions and a two-page attachment that requested additional demographic data, yearly attendance, testing data, and other contextual information. Excluding the additional data sheet, the questionnaire required approximately forty-five minutes to complete.

Qualitative Phase. Even as the quantitative data were being collected, protocols were being designed for the qualitative phase of the study. The purpose of this phase was to gain insight into the human elements that enabled the schools to succeed—those elements that statistics cannot convey. There was the need, for example, to observe firsthand how interpersonal relationships worked, how classes were conducted, how resources were actually used, how the insiders perceived their experiences, and what the school climate was actually like. Observations and interviews were conducted at each school site by the project evaluators over the course of one week. Research protocols were used to guide the evaluation process and included guidelines for whole school and classroom observations and individual and group interview questions specifically targeting administrative personnel, support staff, teachers, parents, and students. Evaluators collected information pertaining to the historical, geographical, and political context of each school.

Schools Targeted for Qualitative Study. The qualitative sample consisted of nine elementary schools selected to represent a cross section of the country. The qualitative data from four schools randomly selected within the geographical area are the focus of this discussion. These four schools were given pseudonyms to reflect the region of the country in which they were located: Eastern Elementary, Midwestern Elementary, Southwestern Elementary, and Farwest Elementary. Each of was situated in an urban area and served a predominantly low-income African American student population.

Findings

We have extracted findings that demonstrate the importance of triangulation and highlight the ways in which triangulation fosters culturally responsive evaluation. The findings can be placed into three broad categories: physical components, school climate, and levels of involvement.

Physical Components. The two components examined here were building quality and resources.

Quality of the Building. The effect of school environment on academic performance has been documented (Learning First Alliance, 2001; Nettles, Mucherah, and Jones, 2000). Quantitative data from the questionnaire indicated that all principals agreed with items stating that their school buildings were clean and attractive, students and teachers took pride in their building, the school was safe and secure during school days, and vandalism by students was not a problem.

Our observations confirmed that the buildings were indeed clean and attractive and that students and teachers took pride in them. What we also discovered, however, was that although principals reported that vandalism by students was not a problem, it did not necessarily mean that vandalism was not a problem at the school. For example, our interviews revealed that Farwest Elementary had a serious and ongoing problem with vandalism perpetrated by outsiders over the weekends. The principal's response to the vandalism question did not reflect the fact that vandalism was not a problem at her school because she, her staff, and the students went to great lengths to ensure that walls and pavements were rid of graffiti and grounds were clear of trash. Much to our surprise over the course of the week in which we visited that school, we saw that school staff, students, and parents were perpetually cleaning walls and picking up garbage left over from a weekend of vandalism. Furthermore, what our quantitative data could never convey was the enormous sense of shared ownership that students had for the school environment. This was a theme that was revealed in each of the student focus group interviews. Students expressed that keeping the school building and grounds clean was far from a burden: it was an activity in which they took great pride.

A similar example of how the questionnaire results provided misleading data can be noted with the issue of playground facilities. We learned from interviews and observations that despite questionnaire data indicating a safe and secure school environment, at two of the schools the lack of playground facilities and a potentially violent surrounding neighborhood posed problems that threatened this safety and security. Again, the principals did not identify these as problems because they had been creative in dealing with such challenges. For example, at one school, playground facilities were built on the rooftop of the school building.

As we collated the data derived from interviews and observations, we gained knowledge about school environment issues we had not anticipated, and this helped us to adjust or add to our existing questionnaire items to address what appeared to be obvious gaps. That is, we added questions that spoke directly to physical environment issues not typically addressed in the literature, such as how students and teachers feel about the areas surrounding the school and whether the school had sufficient recreational areas for students.

Resources. Given that the issue of resource availability is often raised in discussions about the success or failure of high-poverty urban schools serving African American youth (Hammond, 1998), we evaluated the extent to which textbooks, computers, and other resources were present and deemed as essential for student success at these exemplary schools.

The questionnaire asked, "How would you rate the quality of the school's resources?" Midwestern and Farwest principals indicated "excellent" on a four-point scale ranging from 1, "poor," to 4, "excellent." The qualitative data gathered during site visits substantiated these reports. Teachers at Midwestern and Farwest reported that they had everything they needed and more (for example, fiber-optic wiring for in-house Internet services). Eastern and Southwestern principals indicated "good" on the scale, which was not verified by our observations. Our site visits revealed that Southwestern Elementary had few, if any, functioning computers, except in the principal's office, and it had no operational library. Many classes were held in what were originally temporary classrooms (tin-roofed and windowless trailers) that had seemingly become permanent appendages to the main building. In interviews at Southwestern Elementary, teachers expressed some frustration with the lack of resources, but all made positive statements indicating that they maximized the use of resources available to them. Similar findings were obtained at Eastern Elementary. These results clearly suggest that the use of rating scales with response options like "excellent" and "good" provide only crude indicators and leave much room for variation and interpretation.

School Climate. An important factor related to school success is school climate (Witcher, 1993), and this is perhaps the area in which qualitative measures contribute the most (Lindelow and others, 1989). Qualitative evaluations of climate provide deeper insight regarding the relationship between the school's structural components and student behavior. We assessed a number of contextual and structural factors as contributing to school climate, including organizational characteristics, dress codes, and disciplinary policies and practices.

Organizational Characteristics. As stable as one might think organizational characteristics are, we were made emphatically aware of how quickly changes in urban school settings occur and how such changes can significantly affect school personnel, school reform model implementers, and evaluators (Duignan, 1986). Given that the qualitative phase of our study took place a year after the completion of the quantitative phase, we anticipated the minor adjustments we had to make to the data we initially received pertaining to student and teacher populations. What we did not anticipate was that by the time we conducted the site visits, major structural changes had occurred in two of the schools.

By the time we made our site visit to Southwestern Elementary, it no longer had a fifth grade. Furthermore, students from other schools in the district had been transferred to this school, thereby significantly increasing the number of second-grade classrooms. This had serious implications, according to the principal, contributing to a drop in the school's ranking on standardized measures and lowering student morale. In contrast, Midwestern Elementary School profited from an organizational change that added prekindergarten classes. This addition enabled the school to qualify for an increase in funding. Without the follow-up qualitative study, we would have been unaware of changes in organizational characteristics and could have missed important contextual factors threatening or enhancing these schools' status as exemplary schools. These examples illustrate the importance of triangulating data sources and acquiring data over time in order to keep pace with the rapid change that often occurs in the urban school environment.

Dress Code. In gathering information related to the schools' dress codes, we were again faced with seemingly conflicting data. To an apparently straightforward question, "Is a dress code or uniform required at your school?" we found that an affirmative answer did not always mean the same thing across different settings. For example, at Southwestern Elementary, there were several varieties of school uniform, but strict adherence to the code was not demanded. This is an important point because contrary to what a uniform policy usually implies, students at this school did in fact retain a significant amount of choice and control of their dress.

Disciplinary Policies and Practices. With respect to questions specifically related to discipline, we again found many inconsistencies among the principals' reports on the quantitative questionnaires, our on-site observations, and interviews with students, teachers, and parents. For example, questionnaire data indicated that all principals agreed that students treat each other respectfully and are not subject to verbal or physical abuse by other students. However, students at all the schools reported significant amounts of bullying, name-calling, and fighting on school grounds. Even in instances where principals reported a zero-tolerance policy for physical violence, teachers reported a lack of disciplinary follow-through by principals.

A good illustration is reflected in responses to the question related to applying behavior standards fairly and consistently. All principals, except the principal of Midwestern Elementary, strongly agreed with this statement. The principal agreed only with the statement related to applying behavior standards fairly and consistently, but "strongly agreed" with the following statement: "Students appear to believe that school rules are reasonable and appropriate." Yet during our interviews at this school, teachers expressed dismay over the tendency of the principal not to dispense justice fairly and consistently. In addition, students and teachers were extremely unhappy about the strict disciplinary policy that forced students to toe lines painted on the floors in hallways and to be silent in the hallways and in the cafeteria during lunch.

Levels of Involvement. Another domain of investigation pertained to levels of involvement, including parental involvement and site-based management, both cited as important factors related to student achievement in the exemplary schools literature specifically related to disadvantaged populations (ERIC/CUE Digest, 1985; Levine and Lezotte, 1990; Wang, Haertel, and Walberg, 1997).

Parental Involvement. A number of items on the questionnaire addressed parental involvement. With the exception of two areas (helping parents develop literacy skills and assisting parents in helping their children in the transition from home to preschool or kindergarten), all principals gave their school high ratings for parent-school communication and parental involvement. Our observations during the site visits indicated that all the schools were indeed strong on school-parent communications, but that parental involvement in decision making and budgeting was almost nonexistent. Parental involvement was strongest at Eastern Elementary, and this can be attributed to the fact that this school had adopted the School Development Program (Comer, 1980) and had a parent liaison present in the school for most of the week. It should be noted that the School Development Program, developed by James Comer, M.D., is designed to recreate a caring, nurturing, and challenging learning community in which adults work collaboratively to address children's psychosocial and academic development. At the other schools, there were no signs of explicit parent-teacher group contact and there appeared to be only a small number of parents (four or five at most) who played any roles in the school at all.

One principal indicated on the questionnaire that there was a parent resource center at his school. However, our observations indicated that no such center existed. When we spoke with the principal about this, he reported that the school no longer had the center, and it was unclear why it had disappeared. Parents who were called together for our interviews (except in one school, where we were allowed to interview randomly) seemed to know little about overall school governance issues.

Our quantitative data indicating strong parental involvement was clearly not substantiated by our qualitative observations and interviews. An inherent problem seems to be that the questions posed in the questionnaire did not specifically ask about the extent or quality of parent involvement. Notably, however, results from our qualitative phase revealed a diverse set of roles played by those parents who were involved, including assisting teachers, leading classes, supervising playground activities, and, in some cases, fundraising substantial amounts for money for the school. We were also made aware of the fact that the school context can significantly influence the level and form of parental involvement. For example, Southwestern Elementary was located in an extremely depressed neighborhood in which many parents were absent as a result of being incarcerated or in drug treatment programs; hence, many students lived with extended family members or were in foster care. As a result of our interviews, it became clear that questions regarding "parental involvement" needed to have been broader and spoken to "family involvement."

Site-Based Management. Data derived from the questionnaire indicated that the amount of site-based control perceived by the principals varied across schools. However, all principals reported that they had little or no control over the hiring and terminating of staff, but some control over setting school policy, establishing parent involvement programs, creating special programs, and determining and implementing the school's budget.

What stood out for us during the school site visits was the diverse ways in which budgets were used and the varying degrees of stakeholder involvement. Principals showed great initiative in locating monies for programs they deemed important. Funds were used to increase human resources (such as teachers' aides and school nurses) at one school and to implement educational programs and purchase equipment at another. All principals reported that creating the school budget was a cooperative effort in which teachers and parents participated. However, our interviews with teachers indicated otherwise: they often reported that their involvement in creating the school budget was negligible. In two of the schools (Midwestern Elementary and Farwest Elementary), the teachers expressed displeasure with their lack of involvement not only in administrative matters such as budgeting but also in pedagogical ones. Teachers at Midwestern Elementary did acknowledge, however, that the principal ensured that their material resource requests were met. Our on-site observations at the school revealed what was clearly a top-down management system that was not reported by the principal on the questionnaire or during the principal interview.

Additional Findings. Part of our rationale for using data triangulation was to strengthen the validity of our findings. It is therefore important to note that we did not always interpret inconsistencies between the qualitative data obtained during site visits and the questionnaire data as reflecting negatively on the principal's ability to report accurately. That is, we acknowledged that there was possibly a misinterpretation of questions or a need for greater specificity in the questionnaire. For example, in responding to the questionnaire item that read, "Does your school have expanded school services such as health clinics, family support services, counseling, etc.?" all of the principals, with the exception of one (Farwest Elementary) reported yes. Yet during our site visits to the school, we found a part-time nurse, a well-equipped nurses' quarter, an active school counselor, and an extensive free breakfast program. In contrast, while the principal at Southwestern Elementary reported having such facilities, our site visit and interview revealed that he was simply referring to the fact that the school allowed a local church to hold services in the school building. Hence, in our use of a compound question, we were unable to ascertain from the questionnaire data what services were and were not provided. Similarly, a question that asked principals to rank factors that they thought were important to student success, none included counseling or other psychosocial services in the top seven of their list, and yet three schools extensively provided these services and the principals identified them in their interviews as important contributors to their students' overall success. These kinds of disparities make a strong case for mixed-method data gathering.

Triangulation and Culturally Responsive Evaluation

The questionnaire data coupled with our qualitative measures (interviews and observations) facilitated a deeper understanding of potential evaluation issues and opened the door to engaging a TD approach in assessing success indicators in these exemplary urban schools. As we have described this process across the three domain categories of findings, the value of triangulating methodologies has been highlighted, but although implied, we have said little about the relationship between triangulation and culturally responsive evaluation.

Essential to our evaluation of these exemplary schools was a data gathering and interpreting process that involved reconciling information derived from multiple data sources. We felt very much that what appeared to be contradictions in data provided a unique opportunity to engage in discussions that contributed to a much richer understanding of how these exemplary schools operated. However, this opportunity depended heavily on our ability to foster a willingness among stakeholders to engage in critical discussions about the strengths, weaknesses, areas needing improvement, and alternative methods employed in their schools. The degree to which we could establish trusting relationships that could foster these types of frank discussions rested on the successful implementation of the fundamental principles of culturally responsive evaluation.

Culturally responsive evaluation encompasses, among other things, attention to contextual factors (such as characteristics of the neighborhood in which schools are situated), a commitment to the process (such as time spent in schools), and the use of shared cultural knowledge as a means of yielding richness in stakeholders' reports. The need for the last was especially salient in schools in which the school staff were predominantly African American. We found that relationship building was an essential part of the evaluation process at both the Eastern and Farwest schools. Staff members at these schools invited us to their homes for meals, to community events, and even to attend religious functions with them. We gladly attended and found our participation in these events communicated our commitment to the process and facilitated an openness in discussions during our interviews.

With an established basis for trust, our interviews were transformed into a co-construction process with stakeholders (school administrators, teachers, parents, and students), with us challenging each group to consider reporting inconsistencies, help us make sense of our data, and draw meaningful conclusions about factors contributing to the school's success. Some of these interviews yielded important information about the cultural milieu of school neighborhoods and associated cultural practices perceived as the platform on which the schools' success was built (for example, a strong emphasis on religious prayer and activities, the use of discipline, and rules that placed a premium on respect for adults—waiting to be spoken to before speaking, qualifying statements with "ma'am" or "sir," and holding doors open). The broader sociopolitical implications of African American evaluators' studying schools that were successfully educating a predominantly low-income African American student population were also discussed and contributed to an open and knowledge-imparting attitude among interview participants.

In sum, recognizing and placing a premium on relationship building and paying close attention to the human elements of school functioning helped us gain valuable insight about the exemplary schools we set out to evaluate. As we collected data in each of the domains, a central theme kept emerging: success has seemingly less to do with what is actually present at the school and more to do with how its presence or absence is perceived and used by various stakeholders. An example is illustrated in the domain of physical components: the actual availability of resources is less important than the perceptions of whether that lack of availability hinders progress in one school, and in another school the abundance of resources is less important than the extent to which staff feel empowered and involved in the process related to their acquisition.

Conclusions

Co-construction and placing evaluation in the context of the total cultural milieu were critical to the success of the evaluation efforts in the Exemplary Schools project. The project involved quantitative and qualitative methods with evaluators from different disciplines and drawing from sources that included observations and interviews with multiple stakeholders (administrators, teachers, students, and parents). Triangulating data sources, evaluators, and methods significantly enhanced our ability to make sense of our findings and create evaluation instruments that had good validity and reliability. In juxtaposing the quantitative and qualitative data, we were able to obtain insights that neither of the methodologies could yield in isolation.

The Exemplary Schools project assisted CRESPAR in reformatting the way in which we ask questions when evaluating schools. We learned that it is critical to delineate in questionnaires whether we were looking for a statement of opinion or fact. Our observational and interview data often substantiated much of the quantitative data gathered from the questionnaires completed by school principals. Nonetheless, on-site observations and interviews with principals, teachers, parents, and students also revealed discrepancies between the principals' reports and the actual situation. This led us to wonder if some principals' responses reflected what they considered ideal, as opposed to real. This may have not been a question of the principals' providing intentionally misleading information, but a matter of their interpreting the question differently from what we had intended.

We were also made aware of how easy it is to make errors when responding to quantitative questions. A simple illustration is a questionnaire response indicating that both the principal and the assistant principal were male. Much to our surprise, upon arrival, we were met by a female assistant principal, who spoke emphatically about the strengths of having both sexes represented in the administrative role. Believing that both administrators were of the same gender at this school could easily have entered into our analyses and caused us to miss an important aspect of the school's climate or organizational characteristics. Furthermore, despite the fact that most of our questions were specifically drawn from standard measures used in other evaluation studies, we found some unable to capture our outcomes completely and accurately.

While evaluators are often accused of letting their own biases invade their interpretation of qualitative data, we were made patently aware of the fact that quantitative measures can also be limited in the respect that inherent in them are designer biases and ambiguities. By triangulating methodologies, we were made more keenly aware of the potential for drawing incorrect conclusions from what is superficially a clear-cut phenomenon. Hence, the findings of the Exemplary Schools study served its twofold purpose of helping to design a valid and reliable evaluation tool, while stimulating deliberate thought about the efficacy of the principles that undergird the Talent Development Model.

References

Boykin, A. W. "The Talent Development Model of Schooling: Placing Students at Promise for Academic Success." *Journal of Education for Students Placed at Risk,* 2000, 5(1/2), 3–25.

Cole-Henderson, B. "Organizational Characteristics of Schools That Successfully Serve Low-Income, Urban African American Students." *Journal of Education for Students Placed at Risk,* 2000, 5(1/2), 77–91.

Comer, J. *School Power.* New York: Free Press, 1980.

Cuban, L. "Effective Schools: A Friendly But Cautionary Note." *Phi Delta Kappan,* 1983, 64(10), 695–696.

Duignan, P. "Research on Effective Schooling: Some Implications for School Improvement." *Journal of Education Administration,* 1986, 24(1), 59–73.

Edmonds, R. R. *A Discussion of the Literature and Issues Related to Effective Schooling.* Mass.: Urban Education Clearinghouse, 1979. (ED 170 394)

ERIC/CUE Digest. *Parent Participation and the Achievement of Disadvantaged Students.* New York: Clearinghouse on Urban Education, no. 27, 1985.

Flick, U. "Triangulation Revisited: Strategy of Validation or Alternative?" *Journal for the Theory of Social Behavior,* 1992, 22, 175–198.

Greene, J. C., Caracelli, V. J., and Graham, W. F. "Toward a Conceptual Framework for Mixed-Method Evaluation Designs." *Educational Evaluation and Policy Analysis,* 1989, 11, 255–274.

Hammond, A. S. "Standing at the Edge of the Digital Divide." In L. A. Daniels (ed.), *The State of Black America.* Washington, D.C.: National Urban League, 1998.

Jagers, R. J., and Carrol, G. "Issues in Educating African American Children and Youth." In S. Stringfield and D. Land (eds.), *Educating At-Risk Students.* Chicago: National Society for the Study of Education, 2002.

Janesick, V. "The Dance of Qualitative Research Design." In N. Denzin and Y. Lincoln (eds.), *Handbook of Qualitative Research.* Thousand Oaks, Calif.: Sage, 1994.

Learning First Alliance. *Every Child Learning Safe and Supportive Schools.* Washington, D.C.: Association for Supervision and Curriculum Development, 2001.

Levine, D. U., and Lezotte, L. *Unusually Effective Schools: A Review and Analysis of Research and Practice.* Madison, Wis.: National Center for Effective Schools Research and Development, 1990.

Lindelow, J., and others. "School Climate." In S. C. Smith and P. K. Piele (eds.), *School Leadership: Handbook for Excellence.* Eugene, Ore.: Clearinghouse on Educational Management, 1989.

Mace-Matluck, B. *The Effective Schools Movement: Its History and Context.* Austin, Tex.: Southwest Educational Development Lab, 1987.

Nettles, S. M., Mucherah, W., and Jones, D. S. "Understanding Resilience: The Role of Social Resources." *Journal of Education for Students Placed at Risk,* 2000, 5(1/2), 47–60.

Sammons, P., and others. *Key Characteristics of Effective Schools: A Review of School Effectiveness Research.* London: University of London, Institute of Education, 1995.

Stake, R. "Case Studies." In N. Denzin and Y. Lincoln (eds.), *Handbook of Qualitative Research.* Thousand Oaks, Calif.: Sage, 1994.

Stedman, L. C. "A New Look at the Effective Schools Literature." *Urban Education,* 1987, 20(3), 295–326.

Townsend, T. "School Effectiveness: Identifying the Complexities." Paper presented at the annual meeting of the International Congress for School Effectiveness and Improvement, Norrkoping, Sweden, 1993.

Wang, M. C., Haertel, G. D., and Walberg, H. J. "Urban School Effects: A Research Synthesis." Paper presented at the annual meeting of the American Educational Research Association, Chicago, 1997.

Wimpelberg, R. K., Teddlie, C. and Stringfield, S. "Sensitivity to Context: The Past and Future of Effective Schools Research." Paper presented at the annual meeting of the American Educational Research Association, Washington, D.C., April 1987.

Witcher, A. E. "Assessing School Climate: An Important Step for Enhancing School Quality." *NASSP Bulletin,* 1993, 77, 1–5.

Witte, J. F., and Walsh, D. "A Systematic Test of the Effective Schools Model." *Educational Evaluation and Policy Analysis,* 1990, 2(2), 188–212.

DONNA PENN TOWNS is senior research associate with the Center for Research on the Education of Students Placed At Risk, Howard University, Washington, D.C.

ZEWELANJI SERPELL is a consultant with the Center for Research on the Education of Students Placed At Risk, Howard University, and an administrative faculty member at James Madison University, Harrisonburg, Va.

5

This chapter illustrates the importance of a comprehensive professional development evaluation design.

Talent Development Professional Development Evaluation Model: A Paradigm Shift

Constance M. Ellison

Professional development has moved from the periphery of teachers' professional lives to center stage (Roskos and Bain, 1998), clearly recognized today as one of the key factors that shape teachers' ability to reach and teach all students successfully. To be effective, any professional development program must pay close attention to changes in teacher classroom performance, school program and organizational effectiveness, and student learning and achievement outcomes. Professional development programs must be assessed to document their value to the school organization, other educational stakeholders, and ultimately the students. To be comprehensive and authentic over time, professional development efforts need to be accompanied by a well-designed evaluation plan for determining their effectiveness. Such a plan must be accompanied by both a summative and formative evaluation design that provides evidence of the efficiency and effectiveness of program implementation and outcome attainment (Guskey, 2002; Frechtling, 2001; Rice and Powell, 2000). Data yielded from such evaluations can provide educators with information regarding the development of new roles and teaching strategies that will improve student achievement and learning outcomes.

The work reported herein was supported by grant(s) from the Institute of Education Sciences (IES) (formerly the Office of Educational Research and Improvement), U.S. Department of Education. The findings and opinions expressed in this chapter do not necessarily reflect the position or policies of the Institute of Education Sciences or the U.S. Department of Education.

This chapter discusses a professional development program evaluation model consistent with the Talent Development (TD) evaluation framework.

Overview of the Talent Development Professional Development Program

Since 1994, the TD comprehensive school reform paradigm has guided the Center for Research on the Education of Students Placed At Risk (CRESPAR), seeking to transform schools for children who historically have been placed at risk for educational failure (Boykin, 2000). Ongoing, comprehensive professional development is an integral part of CRESPAR's proposition that all children can learn if they are provided with the proper support system. Embracing a co-constructivist approach, professional development as envisioned by the Talent Development Professional Development (TDPD) project refers to sustained strategies and organizational supports that ensure the career development of teachers and others who influence the learning success of students.

An investigation into the literature on professional development shows that there have been many flawed professional development efforts—for example:

- Failure to meet teachers' needs
- Brief and infrequent workshops
- Programs that are not research based and results driven
- Efforts mandated by central administration
- Programs that allow little opportunity for practice, feedback, or follow-up
- The use of outdated in-service training modalities

Research also points to the characteristics of good professional development. To be effective and useful for teachers, professional development efforts must:

- Be results driven and job embedded
- Focus on helping teachers become immersed in subject matter and teaching methods
- Be curriculum centered and standards based
- Be sustained, rigorous, and cumulative
- Be directly linked to what teachers do in their classrooms
- Include co-constructive and collaborative input from teachers
- Be built on teachers' strengths, talents, and assets
- Have an effect on teachers' behavior, attitudes, and knowledge base in the classroom

This approach to professional development differs significantly from more traditional approaches. For too long, professional development activities, embracing a reductionist model, have focused training and evaluation efforts on the development of isolated skills and strategies for improving single aspects of the educational process (Hixson and Tinzmann, 1990). With talent development as its guiding philosophy, the TDPD program articulates the notion that all students can learn by providing professional development activities to educators that are needs driven and school focused and offer a co-constructivist approach to reflective classroom practices.

Unlike many other structured professional development programs, a co-constructivist approach guides TDPD intervention activities, which are both needs driven and school focused. Any professional development program activity should be based on a needs-driven paradigm, responsive specifically to the needs of both teachers and the school. A school-focused professional development paradigm looks specifically at how schools envision their school improvement efforts. Here, there is an effort to determine school-based needs and how they can be met through professional development activities. Our co-constructivist model helps teachers to embrace professional development activities by contextualizing these activities to make implementation easier for their particular sites.

Applying the Talent Development Evaluation Framework to Professional Development

Thomas (Chapter One, this volume) asserts that the Talent Development Model, like any other educational reform program, must empirically test its reform efforts against a consistent set of rigorous standards of evidence. She points out that in order to obtain an accurate picture of how well TD projects such as the TDPD project are doing, evaluations should follow procedures that are systematic, co-constructed, contextually and culturally relevant, responsive, and triangulated. Monitoring and evaluation are clearly essential to improving the effectiveness of TD programs. Careful program monitoring allows TDPD evaluators to make appropriate decisions on a day-to-day basis, and it ensures that programs are carried out as designed or altered when necessary. Evaluation enables TDPD evaluators to understand and demonstrate the results of their work and determine the best strategies for achieving their goals and documenting lessons learned. This discussion of the TDPD evaluation model highlights three features of the TD evaluation framework: cultural context, the use of multiple measures, and co-construction.

Frierson, Hood, and Hughes (2002) have suggested ways of infusing culturally responsive work during each phase of the evaluation process. According to these authors, developing understanding of minority issues, cultures, and contexts increases one's awareness of both the external and internal factors that have an effect on the stated goals of the program being evaluated and contributes to a more valid assessment of the program's overall functioning. Culturally responsive evaluation adopts evaluation strategies that are consistent with the cultural context under examination. In addition, ensuring culturally responsive evaluation requires that evaluators examine culturally relevant indicators that may have a significant impact on results obtained and conclusions reached. It involves awareness of the cultural context in which the evaluation is taking place and an understanding by the evaluator of how a program functions within the context of culturally diverse and similar groups. This also implies that evaluators understand the implications of cultural context on the design of the program being evaluated and know how to collect and interpret outcome information gathered during the evaluation process.

We have recognized in our own work in this area the value of a strong cultural influence on interpretations that can be drawn and conclusions reached based on specific cultural indicators. We have developed professional development interventions that emphasize important cultural specific indicators in our program design, implementation, and evaluation. An example is how TDPD evaluators guide and assess teachers' ability to understand the lived experiences of their students in the classroom context. What has often been articulated in the education system is that there is "one best system" of educating all children. In dispelling this myth, TDPD evaluators, following the principles of the TD Model, guide and assess teachers' knowledge and ability to build on students' assets, strengths, and talents in the learning context.

Cultural sensitivity is a unique dimension of the TDPD evaluation framework. In this context, it refers to a set of academic and interpersonal skills and strategies that evaluator and educational stakeholders share, allowing each group to increase its understanding and appreciation of people's lived experiences. This requires a willingness and ability to draw on culturally based values, traditions, and customs and to work with persons of and from a similar cultural background in developing focused professional development interventions and evaluation strategies. Understanding cultural values and etiquette helps school staff and TDPD evaluators speak and behave in culturally responsive ways.

Clearly, then, an important factor that figures prominently in the TD evaluation framework is context. There is no question that any professional development program should be rigorously evaluated, but a focus should also be placed on evaluators' becoming sensitive to the effects of contextual and supportive factors and indicators on the operations of such programs and the necessity of designing and implementing responsive program evaluations. Contextual indicators describe the social, economic, cultural, and demographic influences on the programs and provide assistance in understanding education within the larger context.

A second area highlighted in the TDPD evaluation process is triangulation. It is the position of CRESPAR evaluators that all evaluations, when looking inside the classroom and school context, must incorporate multiple measures of success. It is at this level of evaluation that the TDPD program employs a multicomponent approach providing high-quality professional development experiences to educators by bringing into strategic alignment a number of successful professional development practices that TDPD staff and participating teachers have co-constructed.

Traditionally, evaluations of educational reform programs have focused on numbers, such as looking at improvements in standardized test scores. On the one hand, improving test scores is certainly critical and represents an easily measured indicator. On the other hand, it is not very easy to measure other essential parts of a good program, such as relationships between students and teachers and between teachers and their peers, fostering the moral and ethical development of teachers and school administrators, issues of teacher attrition and retention, and even allowing teachers time to reflect on day-to-day activities. Although each program must develop its own set of specific evaluation criteria, all programs should consider the broader range of desired outcomes, especially the cultural, social, and emotional development of educational stakeholders such as students, teachers, and the administrative staff. These affective components should be in the foreground as the goals and structure of the program are being set as well as how success is being assessed.

Third, TDPD evaluators digress procedurally from a traditional evaluation framework by operating in a dual role as program designers and program evaluators as they co-construct professional development practices and activities with teachers and administrators. Traditional evaluators, who are often external to the organization being evaluated, typically operate externally in a vacuum, working with prescribed agendas. TDPD evaluators are considerably more participatory in their activities. Cousins and Earl (1992) contend that participatory evaluation is marked by the intention of the evaluator to build evaluation capacity among the stakeholders. Such a framework allows TDPD evaluators not only to assist in co-constructing professional development program activities and their implementation, but also to participate in the development and implementation of the evaluation plan as well. During the early stages of program planning, we have established that evaluation efforts are most effective when evaluators and educational stakeholders work collaboratively to realize the goals of the professional development initiative. It is only when everyone sees, from the beginning of the planning process, the value of using evaluative data for school improvement that evaluators and stakeholders become an integrated team. In this capacity, TDPD evaluators begin to assume multiple roles as program developers and evaluators.

This process helps to generate a greater rapport with the teachers, administrators, and other school personnel. It also provides substantial opportunities to collect more contextually relevant information that ordinarily might have been overlooked, minimized, or ignored. Such ancillary information can provide, for example, insight into a combination of school-related factors accompanying professional development interventions that may influence performance outcomes—for example, timing factors, social climate factors, teacher attrition and retention factors, demographic factors, socioeconomic factors, cultural and contextual factors, and other relevant professional activities in progress at the same time. Such factors underscore the importance of and need to define indicators to monitor ongoing progress in the implementation of TDPD interventions and evaluation agenda. For example, when evaluators observe African American teachers, much in the professional development program under evaluation can be lost long before reaching an appreciation of the merit and worth of what has been observed. At our school sites, nonverbal behaviors such as activity disengagement and body movement in the past may have been treated "as error variance" by evaluators and therefore more than likely ignored.

The TDPD evaluation plan was also designed to address schoolwide educational programs. Five principles, consistent with the TD evaluation framework, guided this TDPD evaluation paradigm:

- Formative evaluation of the development of a program must be central in order to make needed modifications.
- The process of gaining understanding and knowledge must be prominent in the evaluation framework..
- The context and support systems of the program are analyzed.
- Evaluation must take into account the interface among the classroom, schoolwide, and system levels.
- The model takes into account the cultural and contextual pressures regarding educational accountability.

Specific evaluation considerations focus on need, conceptualization, development, implementation, and impact. Implicit within each of these evaluation domains are both process variables and outcomes. Consideration is given to both contextual (for example, teacher retention and attrition) and supportive (for example, administrative support and teacher preparation) factors that may have an impact on the program and program implementation. All of these components are addressed in the evaluation plan's strategies.

The TDPD evaluation plan also describes professional development that is aligned with state content and student performance standards. The National Staff Development Council (NSDC) Standards for Staff Development over the years have been geared toward making staff development more responsive to the learning needs of educators and students. NSDC encourages alignment of professional development with these standards as one of several uses for school districts. Each standard can be used in two primary ways: by individuals seeking to better understand and implement effective staff development practices, and by groups who wish to study and implement the standards to improve the organization's staff development effectiveness (NSDC, 1995). The TDPD intervention program and evaluation use both the individual and group processes.

In addition, an objective of the TDPD evaluation is to measure change. Without systemic evaluation of effort based on hard data, it is virtually impossible to determine if sustained changes have occurred. Professional development intervention activities need ongoing evaluation to ensure that goals are being achieved, needs are being met, and resources are being used wisely. For any professional development evaluation model to be effective and beneficial, precisely what will be evaluated must be defined. TDPD's efforts focus on program needs, teacher needs, and student achievement outcomes. This TDPD program targets three areas of effective professional development: (1) the needs and characteristics of participating teachers; (2) the program characteristics of purposes, structure, content, process, follow-up and outcome; and (3) the organizational characteristics that contribute to or support effective professional development.

The TDPD evaluation model serves to inform and improve the operations at each school site. As such, specific emphasis is placed on four evaluation levels:

- Content, or what teachers should know: What is it that a teacher should know, understand, and be able to do as a result of the professional development intervention activity
- Process, or how teachers come to know: Intervention activities designed to help teachers make sense of the content being presented
- Product, or how teachers demonstrate this knowledge: How teachers demonstrate and extend what they know and understand and what they are able to do about the content in the classroom context
- Context, or where and under what condition should teachers know and understand: The system or culture in which the new skills, strategies, and learning will be implemented

At each of these four intervention levels (content, process, product, and context), great effort is given to their alignment systemically with the conceptual framework for school improvement outlined in each school and district's improvement plan, and co-constructing with educational stakeholders regarding the school's educational agenda and responsiveness to school improvement and reform. Through this process, TDPD program interventions must be assessed to document, for accountability purposes, their significance to the school system, classroom teachers, school administrators and staff, and ultimately the students. To ensure the effectiveness of TDPD professional development program interventions and consistent with the recommendation of the NSDC (1995), we view our evaluation as "an ongoing process that is initiated in the earliest stages of program planning and continued beyond program completion" (p. 7).

Evaluation Process for the Talent Development Professional Development Project

The TDPD program demonstrates the potential of professional development to assist in transforming education and current teacher practices. Our challenge has been to create a comprehensive and rigorous evaluation plan that demonstrates that the intervention efforts have been successful in ensuring that all teachers have adequate access to essential knowledge and the skills they need in assisting their students to reach the high levels of achievement required to succeed. TDPD program interventions have these program evaluation goals:

- Assess improvement in student classroom learning and achievement outcomes as a result of professional development intervention techniques and strategies
- Evaluate how TDPD interventions affect teachers' motivation, attitudes, and knowledge in the classroom
- Enable teachers, administrators, and others to evaluate teachers' expertise and innovations in instructional strategies, curriculum development and enhancement, and other essential elements for teaching to high standards and building on students' assets, talents, and strengths
- Evaluate opportunities for teachers to share knowledge, co-construct knowledge, and connect their learning to the classroom
- Assess the infusion of TD principles and philosophy into teachers' professional development enhancement and classroom practices

At CRESPAR, special emphasis is placed on promoting and strengthening the monitoring and evaluation of all projects by fostering an organizational culture that integrates evaluation into all aspects of project planning and development. This approach creates opportunities to use data to inform future programming on an ongoing basis, measure the effect of each project on its intended beneficiaries, and replicate successful strategies. The primary unit of analysis for the TDPD evaluation model is school change and successful student outcomes. However, change at the school level poses some overwhelming challenges to those who seek to measure and evaluate it. This is especially true when the evaluation aspires to attribute changes in teacher attitudes, behaviors, and student academic performance to specific interventions such as the professional development efforts. Not underestimating these important challenges, the following represents one evaluation approach for the TDPD effort. This strategy is framed as a three-stage investigation: (1) the context of the TDPD project, (2) the process by which it is implemented at the school level, and (3) the outcomes of the project.

Context. In this age of concerted attempts to launch evidence-based professional development intervention programs to effect change in teacher classroom behaviors, any evaluation of a professional development school change initiative should begin by describing how this professional development project fits and is fitted into the existing structure and organization of the school and district. At the school level, TDPD evaluators meet with the school's administrators to determine how the effort conforms to the conceptual framework of the school's professional development plan. At these meetings, TDPD staff members co-construct with the administrative staff an agenda of existing professional development needs in the school.

TDPD program evaluators review school (school improvement plans) and district (school standards and district-wide professional development initiatives) documents. They conduct interviews with district staff and perform focus groups with teachers and administrators. In addition, professional development needs are determined and customized to the school's context based on data obtained from a needs assessment inventory that teachers complete at the beginning of each academic year. The TDPD program evaluation staff also conduct classroom observations. These activities are conducted to ascertain how the TDPD program and evaluation plan correspond to the full agenda of school and school system innovations, and specifically to existing staff development provisions. This co-creation discussion occurs at regular intervals of program implementation to ensure that the TDPD program interventions do not drift from the theory that grounds the TD approach.

Process. The implementation of the TDPD professional development evaluation model begins with the participation of teachers in TDPD workshops typically presented at the school site. For evaluation purposes, activity measures of teachers' participation in workshops are taken regularly at each workshop. At the initiation of the project, baseline information is gathered through interviews, surveys, and needs assessments in order to create a more holistic picture of the school sites. Prior to the evaluation team's visit to each school, the school principal identifies key stakeholders for interview, such as teachers and administrators who are knowledgeable about the school and the future needs. Through on-site observations and interviews, evaluators collect information on the status of existing teaching practices. This information is essential to beginning (and ultimately completing) a comprehensive evaluation of the program. In addition, surveys are distributed seeking information on the background characteristics of the teachers, their goals and motivations for participating in the workshops, and their satisfaction with and perceptions of the workshop content and activities.

Another element of the implementation process assesses the school principal's support for and participation in the TDPD project initiatives. This interaction figures significantly in the success of any program. Lessons learned over the years have demonstrated two important concerns in this domain. One is that without principal buy-in, there is little to no support from the school at large. Second, if the buy-in from the school is dictated (or mandated) by the principal independent of the teaching staff, there is little to no teacher support.

The focus of the TDPD implementation evaluation component centers on five levels of analysis: grade level, behavioral objectives for the students, behavioral objectives for the teachers, task objectives, and standardized test outcomes and objectives. Here, an attempt is made to evaluate the extent to which TDPD supports schoolwide improvement goals. This requires a careful, systematic integration of school improvement and professional development plans and goals. For example, if a school's goal is to increase teachers' classroom performance in the areas of mathematics and reading, the TDPD staff co-constructs classroom resources and materials with the teachers to increase their exposure to and engagement with instructional methods that would enable them to pursue that goal.

Prior to this process, preintervention classroom observations are conducted to evaluate the level of support that each teacher needs. Following the intervention, postintervention observations are conducted to determine the impact of the intervention strategies. Teachers have noted in surveys that the co-construction process is extremely beneficial because it allows them to create instructional and curriculum materials that are more suited for their individual classroom purposes, which provides them a certain level of classroom empowerment. All classroom observation protocols and surveys portray, to a great extent, TD principles and philosophies relative to the indicators of success as specified by the TDPD evaluation model. Such indicators include building on students' strengths, talents, and assets. For teachers, indicators for success would be assessing their reflective practice skills and strategies and their impact on teachers' instructional and pedagogical behaviors, as well as their ability to co-construct learning activities that may have an impact on student achievement for infusion in the classroom context.

Outcomes. Outcomes for the TDPD program are examined by evaluating the following:

- Teachers' participation and satisfaction rates
- Teacher co-constructed classroom activities and resources
- The effect on student achievement as measured by school, state, and district assessments
- Changes in teachers' classroom motivation, beliefs, and attitudes toward institutionalization of professional development activities
- Documentation of collaboration among teachers, their peers, and program staff members

The success of all TDPD programs centers on the degree to which the program can promote observable changes in educational practices and student academic success. The outcome portion of the evaluation is focused largely toward the ultimate goal of improved school performance. This is measured by changes in attitudes and behaviors exhibited by both teachers and the principal. For example, rooted in the TDPD evaluation model is the notion of teachers' expectations for student success, their own sense of professional efficacy, teacher motivation, and measurable growth in teaching strategies and skills, as well as the overdetermination of student academic success. Thus, these concepts are embedded in the teacher instructional reflection perception survey. In addition, measurable concepts of growth in teaching strategies and skills as well as the overdetermination of student academic success are infused in the teacher perception of student performance measure.

The TDPD evaluation framework also addresses the possibility of institutionalization of critical program components. For example, interviews with teachers and administrators at the participating school sites are used to gather information about plans for and likelihood of sustainability of the program's classroom interventions. These interviews also determine the extent of infusion of the program's principles of design, analysis, and implementation of innovative classroom practices.

Finally, a major priority of a professional development strategic plan for the TDPD evaluation program plan is the continual monitoring, assessment, and evaluation of the value added of TDPD professional development activities and initiatives. First, a value-added approach involves both formative and summative evaluation of major professional development activities to determine their level of implementation at the school level and their impact on student achievement, teacher performance, and school productivity (Thomas, 2000). A value-added approach is grounded in research. Such an approach quickly pinpoints improvement areas by using a systematic source of data for decision making (Thomas, 2000). Most important, a value-added approach builds shared visions of program quality. Second, aligned with systemic priorities and goals of the school, evaluation assists in monitoring professional development efforts by emphasizing the contribution of professional development initiatives to the achievement of systemic goals articulated in the school improvement plan. This is done by using effective evidence-based instructional strategies and practices and by creating new school structures and programs to enhance the achievement of all students. In addition, TDPD provides a comprehensive assessment and program evaluation process to reinforce the use of research-based best practices in all schools.

Talent Development Professional Development Evaluation Methodology

Professional development is a field in which definitive research on what is effective must be ongoing and comprehensive (O'Neil, 1994; Sparks and Hirsch, 1997). It is too complex to understand by asking simple questions. Any professional development effort must be guided by an overarching, data-driven goal. Data-driven information must be applicable, useful, and practical. Data are likely to be relevant and pertinent if evaluators and stakeholders (especially teachers and school administrators and staff) work collaboratively to identify and co-construct the kinds of information that can be most effectively and efficiently used. Data collection must be purposeful as well. At the school level, evaluators must collect only data that are likely to inform decision making about how to improve the education process.

The ultimate goal of the TDPD evaluation model is to strive toward better results. After the planning and implementation work is done, we need to demonstrate successes and identify areas for improvement on a continual basis. Measuring progress, being accountable for results, and making changes based on reliable data are vital aspects of continual schoolwide improvement. As such, the TDPD evaluation team employs a triangulated or multimixed methodology using a wide variety of quantitative and qualitative methods. Qualitative data sources include, but are not limited to, structured interviews and classroom observations. Quantitative data sources include, but are not limited to, surveys and questionnaires created by the TDPD program staff, state and local assessment test results, and other performance assessments for students. Multiple sources of information to guide improvement and demonstrate impact are used. For example, the TDPD team conducts a needs assessment to determine the focus of the professional development activity, revisiting those needs during the evaluation process to determine if progress has been made toward that end.

TDPD staff created an evaluation team charged with determining the purpose, scope, and tools to be used for the evaluation. A variety of tools to determine the success of the professional development effort are used—for example, peer observation and administrative observation interviews, self-assessment instruments, and analysis of records (such as minutes of faculty meetings)—to evaluate if professional development activities are being translated into valuable classroom activities. In addition, a process has been created in which teachers feel free to critically assess their own practice. Some scholars (see McConney, Rudd, and Ayres, 2002) have criticized such methods, indicating that they yield incongruent results and that evaluators may find themselves reporting conflicting findings. However, in our work, we have found triangulated methods very helpful and insightful in the reporting of empirical findings. In addition, multimixed methods have quite recently become established as a common practice in program evaluation (Caracelli and Greene, 1993; Frechtling and Sharp, 1997; Jick, 1983; McConney, Rudd, and Ayres, 2002).

Challenges Faced and Lessons Learned

As can be gleaned from our efforts to date, we believe the development, implementation, and dissemination of the TDPD program has gone reasonably well and as planned. We are, however, confronted with two challenges that may have a significant impact on evaluation efforts and results. First and foremost is the issue of when to initiate the evaluation process for assessing professional development programs. If, for example, the ultimate assessment of any professional development program is its ability to change the learning context, then the major purpose of evaluating professional development programs is to establish if that change needs to be made to guarantee that change does occur. Yet in some cases, planning for the evaluation of professional development programs sometimes is done as an addendum to the plan. This can cause major challenges to educational program development, implementation, and impact. From our own lessons learned, it is vitally important to think through and design the evaluation process at the beginning of the program rather than tag it on as an afterthought. As we have learned, the evaluation plan is critical from the beginning to determine the evaluation's stakeholders, the learning context, and the responsiveness of all those who will be involved in the process. Thus, for TDPD evaluators, we use the stakeholders (for example, teachers, school administrators, and central administrators) and their interests, the learning context, and stakeholder responsiveness to drive both the approach and the tools used in the evaluation.

Another major challenge experienced in the implementation of TDPD evaluation activities includes getting the leadership in schools to recognize how their leadership style affects the program evaluation process. School administrators need to accept the reality that their behavior indirectly affects everything that goes on in a school and may have a significant impact on teachers' behavior in the evaluation process. One classic example of this happens when the school principal is present when evaluation tools are being disseminated to teachers after the implementation of a professional development activity. Teachers feel obligated to provide to the evaluator socially desirable responses based on what they perceive to be the principal's intentions and agenda in this endeavor. TDPD evaluators spend a considerable amount of time trying to convince teachers that they will not be judged on the basis of success or failure of a professional development training activity or their evaluative responses relative to the activity. In doing so, TDPD evaluators strive to maintain lines of communication that are open and honest in addition to building a positive professional working relationship with both teachers and school administrators to ensure that the evaluation process is both meaningful and beneficial. This is another example of how our evaluation process is unique, emphasizing relationship building and co-constructing efforts. Traditional evaluators are frequently not involved in the development of the professional development activities while at the same time engaged in the evaluation of the intervention. The benefit of a dual role in this process speaks to how evaluators can help to affect the culture of the school environment by being closely tied to the process as well as to the educational stakeholders. In addition, in instances of an intimate evaluator, the educational stakeholders are generally more responsive to the intervention being initiated and are more willing to see it through.

Despite these challenges, there were invaluable lessons learned during this process. For example, we found that teachers were extremely reluctant to commit or be responsive to professional development interventions and evaluation activities that require work above and beyond their regular school routine. Thus, if the teachers perceive the TDPD projects activities as extra work, they are unlikely to participate or participation is at a minimum. Similarly, buy-in for a co-constructed activity on the part of the stakeholders such as the superintendent or principal of a school does not necessarily mean that teachers in that school have bought into the involvement with a particular professional development program. Stakeholder (teacher, administrative staff, principal) buy-in at all levels is extremely important to the success and longevity of professional development programs. Prior to the implementation of any initial TDPD program interventions and evaluation activities, teachers must be provided with an opportunity for thorough discussion about the intervention and evaluation activities. For the TDPD, we ask that a vote be taken at the school site to assess stakeholders' desire for our professional development interventions, and we seek at least a 90 percent buy-in from the teachers and the school administrative staff. If the buy-in is less than 90 percent, the school is not selected to participate in the TDPD program.

It has also been our experience that if the school's timetable or culture does not allow time for or encourage teacher collaboration, a core element of the TDPD program, it is extremely difficult to formulate a partnership with that school. Our experience as educational evaluators suggests that evaluation is most successful when evaluators and school stakeholders work collaboratively to understand the goals of the program. Only when everyone sees the value of using evaluative data for school improvement do evaluators and stakeholders become a collaborative team.

Conclusions

School reform efforts to date demand that schools become places of excellence for all teachers and students. Although the responsibility for improved schooling must be shared and co-constructed among all stakeholders, such as school administrators, teachers, parents, and students, school reform efforts place a tremendous weight especially on teachers (Clair, Adger, Short, and Millen, 1998; Darling-Hammond, 1990). Clearly, professional development plays a role in equipping schools to meet the challenges facing teachers and others responsible for educating students. Teachers, more so than ever before, are being placed in situations where the needed skills and abilities as teachers are, to some extent, beyond what they were taught to do in the classroom context. As a result, this places great responsibility on any professional development program to ensure that training and skills development is seen as a priority. From an evaluation standpoint, efforts must be made to assess whether participation in the professional development activities promotes successful teacher classroom engagement and behaviors and whether student classroom performance improves as a result of such classroom interventions.

As part of a continuous effort of the TDPD, the evaluation plan discussed in this chapter will guide all of our activities in the quest for program improvement. Clearly, moving in this direction is consistent with the growing trend in the education domain. The increased demand for evaluation in education has not only challenged and redirected the way we do things, but it has held education evaluations to a higher standard than before. Although we continue to ask the simple questions, we are triangulating data sources (for example, people, places, and things) and methods (qualitative and quantitative) to balance both process and outcome concerns. In addition to these new trends in educational evaluation, a more concentrated importance has been placed on context. The underlying premise for the evaluation must always be to maximize students' achievement, and to do this, we must understand the context in which program stakeholders learn and live. Educational reform programs should be rigorously evaluated, and a focus should also be placed on evaluators' becoming contextually responsive or sensitive to the contextual factors influencing the behavior of people in programs.

References

Boykin, A. W. "The Talent Development Model of Schooling: Placing Students at Promise for Academic Success." *Journal of Education of Students Placed at Risk,* 2000, 5(1/2), 3–25.

Caracelli, V. J., and Greene, J. C. "Data Analysis Strategies for Mixed-Method Evaluation Designs." *Educational Evaluation and Policy Analysis,* 1993, 5(2), 195–207.

Clair, N., Adger, C., Short, D., and Millen, E. *Implementing Standards with English Language Learners: Initial Findings from Four Middle Schools.* Providence, RI: Northeast and Islands Regional Educational Laboratory, Brown University, 1998.

Cousins, J. B., and Earl, L. M. "The Case for Participatory Evaluation." *Educational Evaluation and Policy Analysis,* 1992, 14(4), 397–418.

Darling-Hammond, L. "Teacher Professionalism: Why and How." In A. Liberman (ed.), *Schools as Collaborative Cultures.* Bristol, Pa.: Falmer Press, 1990.

Frechtling, J. "What Evaluation Tells Us About Professional Development Programs in Mathematics and Science." 2001. [http://SearchERIC.org/ericdc/ED465587.htm].

Frechtling, J., and Sharp, L. *User-Friendly Handbook for Mixed-Method Evaluations.* Arlington, Va.: National Science Foundation, 1997.

Frierson, H., Hood, S., and Hughes, G. "Strategies That Address Culturally Responsive Evaluation." In J. Frechtling (ed.), *The 2002 User-Friendly Handbook for Project Evaluation.* Arlington, Va.: National Science Foundation, 2002.

Guskey, T. R. "Does It Make a Difference? Evaluating Professional Development." *Educational Leadership,* 2002, 59(6), 45–51.

Hixson, J., and Tinzmann, M. B. "Who Are the At-Risk Students of the 1990s?" 1990. [http://www.ncrel.org/sdrs/areas/rpl_esys/equity.htm#d=29].

Jick, T. D. "Mixing Qualitative and Quantitative Methods: Triangulation in Action." In J. Van Maanen (ed.), *Qualitative Methodology.* Thousand Oaks, Calif.: Sage, 1983.

McConney, A., Rudd, A., and Ayres, R. "Getting to the Bottom Line: A Method for Synthesizing Findings Within Mixed-Method Program Evaluation." *American Journal of Evaluation,* 2002, 23(2), 121–140.

National Staff Development Council. *Standards for Staff Development: High School Edition.* Oxford, Ohio: National Staff Development Council, 1995.

O'Neil, J. "Aiming for New Outcomes: The Promise and the Reality." *Educational Leadership,* 1994, *51*(6), 6–10.

Rice, K. E., and Powell, K. R. "Assessing Student Perceptions of Classroom Methods and Activities in the Context of an Outcomes-Based Evaluation." *Evaluation Review,* 2000, *24*(6), 635–646.

Roskos, K., and Bain, R. "Professional Development as Intellectual Activity: Features of the Learning and Environment and Evidence of Teachers' Intellectual Engagement." *Teacher Educator,* 1998, *34*(2), 89–115.

Sparks, D., and Hirsch, S. *A New Vision for Staff Development.* Alexandria, Va.: Association for Supervision and Curriculum Development, 1997.

Stufflebeam, D. L. "The Relevance of the CIPP Evaluation Model for Educational Accountability." *Journal of Research and Development in Education,* 1971, *5*(1), 19–25.

Thomas, V. G. "Talent Development School Reform Evaluation Guide: Understanding and Framing Talent Development School Reform Evaluation Efforts." Unpublished manuscript, 2000.

CONSTANCE M. ELLISON is principal investigator of the Talent Development Professional Development Project at the Howard University Center for Research on the Education of Students Placed At Risk (CRESPAR) and associate professor, Department of Human Development and Psychoeducational Studies, School of Education, Howard University, Washington, D.C.

6

This commentary discusses the extent to which the CRESPAR evaluation case examples provided in this volume demonstrate a coherent application of the Talent Development evaluation framework.

Commentary: Do Talent Development Project Evaluations Demonstrate a Coherent Approach?

Floraline I. Stevens

In Chapter One of this volume, Thomas emphasizes that the Talent Development (TD) Model is an alternative approach to urban school reform in that it addresses issues previously ignored by other reform projects. That is, cultural and contextual issues are viewed and treated as important elements of the reform rather than being ignored or minimized. The model focuses on the possibilities of success for urban students generally viewed as sure candidates for failure. The model asserts that all students can learn to high standards when key stakeholders are committed to such a goal and hold themselves to high standards. This programmatic approach is clearly a paradigm shift: the model moves much of the responsibility for success from the student to the adult stakeholders who are the program developers, program implementers, evaluators, school administrators, teachers, parents, and community persons.

Talent Development Model and Talent Development Evaluation Model

The TD Model specifies six dimensions on which TD projects and interventions are developed:

- Building on students' assets
- Providing students with transitional support across key development periods in their lives

- Engaging students in constructivist and activist learning
- Preparing students for skill and careers for the twenty-first century
- Promoting the concept of school as community
- Focusing on meaning and connected learning

TD projects are expected to educate the whole child. Across these six dimensions, the TD projects and interventions must rely on more than test scores as evidence of success.

Thomas in Chapter One reminds us that because of the goal and philosophy of the TD Model, the evaluation framework for TD interventions is quite ambitious. This requires ongoing evaluations that seek to inform about the multiple purposes and perspectives of the interventions. Through these varied types of evaluations (developmental, transformative, outcome, knowledge development, and others), TD evaluators hope their evaluations will yield the varied types of information to provide a profound understanding of urban education, its students, and its contexts; help strengthen students and urban schools; enlighten and empower those who have been oppressed and marginalized in school systems; and examine the worth, productivity, and value of school reform efforts.

Criteria for Demonstrated Coherence of the TD Evaluation Framework

As an independent evaluator not affiliated with the Howard University Center for Research on the Education of Students Placed At Risk (CRESPAR), I was asked to review the introductory chapter and the four case evaluations described in this volume. My role in providing this commentary is to discuss the extent to which the case examples demonstrate a coherent approach guided by the TD evaluation framework derived from the TD Model of School Reform. I will assess the coherence by using the descriptions of the five overlapping themes central to the design and implementation of the evaluators. The themes' procedures rely heavily on the relationships established by the TD evaluator with urban school stakeholders. The major difference found in the TD evaluation framework compared to other evaluation frameworks is the prominent roles given to urban school stakeholders. Rather than the perfunctory or marginal contacts made by evaluators with stakeholders, usually at the beginning and end of the evaluations, TD evaluators are strongly encouraged to have positive, respectful, and ongoing contacts and communications with urban school stakeholders. The TD evaluation themes—engaging stakeholders, co-construction, responsiveness, cultural and contextual relevance, and triangulation of perspectives—respond to the notion that stakeholders' continuous involvement in the evaluation is imperative to both the evaluation's success and TD project success. These themes are comprehensively defined in Chapter One; briefer definitions follow:

• *Engaging stakeholders.* Stakeholders must be engaged in authentic ways throughout the evaluation. It is necessary to gain access to and get the cooperation of different stakeholder groups (students, parents, teachers, and other school personnel) to frame the right evaluation questions and implement an appropriate methodology. TD evaluators must provide stakeholders with multiple opportunities to ask questions, critique their efforts, and participate in various ways. TD evaluators must attempt to get to know the school, its students, staff, parents, and surrounding community prior to the implementation of any interventions and evaluations.

• *Co-construction.* This is a process of respecting the social and cultural dynamics of students, families, teachers, and other school personnel that affect learning to ensure that these stakeholders have authentic input into the learning process. Time and effort are required to acquire a shared vision between the TD evaluators and urban school stakeholders. The evaluators and key stakeholders must become ongoing partners and collaborators, jointly framing questions, methodologies, and strategies for dissemination of findings.

• *Responsiveness.* TD evaluators must focus on the people whose programs are under review. They must consider the urban school stakeholders' perspectives prior to planning, implementing, and evaluating any intervention. They also must respect, honor, attend to, and represent stakeholders' perspectives.

• *Cultural and contextual relevance.* Culture (the shared values, traditions, norms, customs, arts, history, folklore, and institutions of a group of people) should be an essential aspect of any meaningful urban school programmatic research and policy agenda. Cultural competence involves having the skills that allow TD evaluators to increase their understanding and appreciation of cultural differences and similarities within, among, and between groups and having the willingness to draw on community values, traditions, and customs.

Context includes the totality of the environment in which the project takes place. A TD evaluator remembers and respects context as the combination of culture and other factors that accompany the implementation and evaluation of a project that might influence results, including geographical location, timing, political and social climate, economic conditions, and other things going on at the same time as the project.

• *Triangulation of perspectives.* The TD evaluator uses both quantitative and qualitative data in a single study or multiple studies of a sustained program of research on a particular phenomenon. Evaluations have several forms of triangulation: investigator triangulation (having a research team with diverse perspectives and areas of expertise), multiple operations (using different ways to measure a single concept), methodological triangulation (using multiple data collection techniques that assess different dimensions of a problem), target person triangulation (collecting data from more than one person on a particular issue), and analysis triangulation (using more than one strategy or statistical technique to analyze the same data).

I used these themes to determine whether there was coherence to the TD evaluation framework. From the chapter titles, I knew that three of the chapters had a key theme: Chapter Two on co-construction, Chapter Three on cultural responsiveness, and Chapter Four on methodology triangulation. Chapter Five focused on the theme of co-construction, but its title gave no indication of this being the major theme. The contents of the five overlapping themes were used as the criteria for determining the evaluations' adherence to the TD evaluation framework.

Therefore, the question of a coherent approach is guided by the TD evaluation framework and is twofold: first, whether the description of the implementation of each chapter's key theme is aligned or coherent with the criteria previously described as essential for a TD evaluation; and second, although each evaluation may have a key theme, whether the evaluation as described also attends to other valued TD evaluation themes.

A Demonstrated Coherent Approach

Examining the narrative in each of the chapters, I was able to determine which and how many of the themes adhered to the TD evaluation framework's themes. From Table 6.1, it is evident that the evaluations were coherent with the TD evaluation framework themes derived from the TD goals and philosophy.

All of the chapters' key themes had extensive narrative describing the evaluation procedures. The case examples discussed by Butty, Reid, and LaPoint (Chapter Three) and Ellison (Chapter Five) covered all of the five themes of the TD evaluation framework. The case examples discussed by

Table 6.1. Presence of Talent Development Evaluation Framework Themes

Themes	Chapter Focuses			
	Two: Co-Construction	Three: Culturally Responsive	Four: Triangulating Methodologies	Five: TD Professional Development
Engaging stakeholders	X	X	X?	X
Co-construction	**X**	X	X?	**X**
Responsiveness	X	**X**		X
Cultural and contextual relevance	X	**X**	X	X
Triangulation		X	**X**	X

Note: A bold **X** denotes the chapter's key theme. X? denotes that there were very limited procedural descriptions of the process.

LaPoint and Jackson (Chapter Two) and Towns and Serpell (Chapter Four) covered four of the five themes. LaPoint and Jackson did not include triangulation, and Towns and Serpell did not include responsiveness in its narrative in sufficient detail. Also, Towns and Serpell had two themes (engaging stakeholders and co-construction) that were mentioned but had limited descriptive narrative of the evaluation procedures that aligned them to the themes.

Conclusion

Thomas in Chapter One provides the research-based grounding for the TD evaluation framework. This information was used to determine whether there was coherence between TD evaluations described in this volume with the TD evaluation framework. In general, the findings showed coherence. Varying amounts of procedural descriptions of the themes used in the TD projects and interventions were provided. However, after reviewing the case examples presented in this volume, I am concerned that the TD goal that all children can learn to high standards was not addressed by the TD evaluations discussed in this volume. No chapter addresses teaching and learning in urban classrooms and how the TD impact was evaluated. In other words, how do engaging stakeholders, co-construction, responsiveness, cultural and contextual relevance, and triangulation play out in relation to evaluating teaching and learning in classrooms composed of urban school students who are at risk of failing?

In Chapter One, Thomas reminds us that the TD interventions seek to educate the whole child. I agree that it is good that TD does not solely focus on raising students' test scores on standardized achievement measures. But I cannot escape the fact that the real world values and gives merit to projects and interventions that raise students' achievement scores. I also agree that other measures and findings are important to report in evaluations. When investigating the themes derived from the TD goals and philosophy, the evaluations need to address the following:

- *Engaging stakeholders.* When framing the right questions, the academic achievement of the students should be a major issue. Students, parents, and school personnel want students to improve, not fail.
- *Co-construction.* This process should affect students' learning, and the stakeholders should have authentic input in the learning process."
- *Cultural and contextual relevance.* To combat urban students' indifference to learning, attention and respect must be paid to their cultural backgrounds and the environments in which they must function and survive. Particular learning strategies that are culture based need to be included in the TD projects and interventions.
- *Responsiveness.* Evaluators have the responsibility of sharing information about outcomes that have a positive impact on student academic

achievement. TD projects and interventions have to address academic achievement interventions as well as the support interventions to be able to provide this type of information.

• *Triangulation.* Data accumulated from mixed methods and multiple perspectives should allow for more complex analyses that help predict what variables when combined produce improved academic achievement for students.

Academic achievement data, coupled with impact information from the evaluations that used the TD evaluation framework of engaging stakeholders, co-construction, responsiveness, cultural and contextual relevance, and triangulation of perspectives are critical to provide powerful support for the concept of talent development of students placed at risk for academic failure.

FLORALINE I. STEVENS is president of Stevens and Associates, an evaluation and research consulting firm in Pasadena, California.

This commentary explores the utility of critical race theory in the evaluation process in education, particularly in regard to the methodological and epistemological perspectives put forth by the Talent Development evaluation paradigm.

Commentary: Can Critical Theories of or on Race Be Used in Evaluation Research in Education?

Laurence Parker

Critical race theory (CRT), as a critique of racism in the law and society, emerged as an outgrowth of the critical legal studies movement that took place at Harvard Law School and the University of California, Berkeley, Law School in the early 1980s (Crenshaw, 2002; Lawrence, 2002). The law professors and students in this group began to question the objective rationalist nature of the law and the process of adjudication in the U.S. legal system. They criticized the way in which the real effects of the law served to privilege the wealthy and powerful in U.S. society while having a deleterious impact on the rights of the poor to use the courts as a means of redress. Out of this growing critique of the role of law in society, a strand of critical scholarship emerged through the writings of Derrick Bell, Mari Matsuda, Richard Delgado, Angela Harris, and Kimberlie Crenshaw (see discussions by Crenshaw, Gotanda, Peller, and Thomas, 1995; Delgado and Stefancic, 2000). These scholars argued that the critical legal studies movement did not go far enough in challenging the racialized nature of the law and its impact on persons of color.

Overview and Roots of Critical Race Theory

The early critical race theorists made several distinct legal and social commentary claims that pointed their critique of the epistemology of law and legal practice. One point stressed was that racism is a normal daily fact of life in society, and the ideology and assumptions of racism are so ingrained in the political and legal structures as to be almost unrecognizable. Legal racial designations have complex historical and socially constructed meanings that ensure the location of political superiority of racially marginalized groups. As a form of oppositional scholarship, CRT challenges the experience of white European Americans as the normative standard. Rather, CRT grounds its conceptual framework in the distinctive contextual experiences of people of color and racial oppression through the use of literary narrative knowledge and storytelling to challenge the existing social construction of race. CRT attacks liberalism and the inherent belief in the law to create an equitable, just society. Furthermore, CRT advocates point out the legal racial irony and liberal contradiction of the frustrating legal pace of meaningful reform that has eliminated blatant hateful expressions of racism, yet kept intact exclusionary relations of power as exemplified by the conservative backlash of the courts, legislative bodies, voters, and others against special rights for racially marginalized groups.

Critical race theorists argued that the law, particularly civil rights law of the 1960s, was targeted to combat classical racism. This type of racism was characterized by acts such as grossly offensive behavior toward others because of their race, legal segregation and discrimination by public bodies, and overt acts of racial violence. The moral authority of the civil rights movement served to weaken this form of racism in the United States, and the power of the law was a vital tool in helping to eliminate classical racism; most white European Americans now abhor these actions against any racial group. However, one of the main tenets of CRT has been that while classical racism has subsided, everyday racism has remained alive. This type of racism can be characterized as those mundane practices and events that are infused with varying degrees of racism. The actions associated with everyday racism are subtle, automatic, nonverbal exchanges that are seen as derogatory slights by African Americans. Furthermore, everyday racism, in the form of micro aggression, is incessant and cumulative as practiced in everyday actions by individuals, groups, and institutional policy rules and administrative procedures. Critical race theory sought to expose the flaws in the color-blind view of everyday social relations and the administering of law by positing that the legal hope of ending discrimination and racism has not made a difference; there is a contradiction in a professed belief in equality and justice, but a societal willingness to tolerate and accept racial inequality and inequity (Tate, 1997; Ladson-Billings, 1998).

The roots of CRT can be partially traced to previous social science race-based critiques related to the epistemological and ontological construction of race and racialism within modernity (Parker, Deyhle, and Villenas, 1999; Parker and Lynn, 2002; Lopez and Parker, 2003). The legal theories related to race share commonalities with other critical theoretical positions related to race and history, philosophy, and the social sciences. For example, in order to understand modernity and its evolution, one has to understand race, racialism, and how race played a fundamental role in shaping philosophical, political, and, later, scientific thought (Goldberg,

1993). In race-centered nation-states (for example, the United States, United Kingdom, South Africa, and Brazil), the sociological myth of racial categories is a powerful primary socialization tool that has a tremendous impact on social perceptions, social status, and the social identity of all societal members (Stanfield, 1999).

Racial categorization is a part of cognitive psychological thinking in that it refers to the ways people think about humans defined in terms of race (McMorris, 1996). It links social and cultural attributes to visible physical attributes. Therefore, reasoning is based on racial categories, and it is more or less commonly accepted along with the rhetoric of progressive social justice through color-blindness and acceptance of all that is used as a pretext to continue to justify hierarchical racial categories. Racial micro aggression also continues on traditionally white college campuses by creating differing degrees of hostile environmental encounters for African Americans that result in "cumulative racism," or a convergence of all the subtle yet still prejudicial put-downs or actions that groups such as African Americans, Latinos and Latinas, Chicanos and Chicanas, and Asian/Pacific Island Americans experience on these campuses because of their race (Feagin, 1992). All of these examples are illustrative of how other critical research centering on race connects to CRT, resulting in a powerful and encompassing framework of racial theory from a critical interdisciplinary perspective.

Given the critical race-based positions that were developed in other fields, their coupling with CRT has given the theory expanding explanatory power to address the myriad elements of race, their role in shaping law and the nation state, personal and group identity, distribution of goods and services, and institutional practices and policies. Since its inception, CRT has not locked itself into a singular line of criticism against the law and society regarding race (Hayman, 1995). CRT has evolved from its early focus on African Americans and the impact of the law on black-white European American relations, to examining how issues related to the law and immigration, national origin, language, globalization, and colonization related to race. From this line of critique formed the LatCrit and critical Asian American legal studies movement that called for a type of critical race theory specific to these groups of color. For example, LatCrit has drawn similarities with CRT regarding racism within U.S. law. Yet the LatCrit movement sees itself grounded more in documenting through narrative storytelling how other aspects of race, ethnicity, language, and national origin converge to make it so that Latinos and Latinas are seen as other within the U.S. racial context (Iglesias, 1999). Asian American CRT uses the power of narrative voice and how it can inform the law regarding the Asian American experience. For example, the work of Chon (1995) and Chartier (2001) stresses the importance of narrative and storytelling to use in a critical reading and tracing of the use of language and discourse and the law to create a climate of discrimination through setting up Asian Americans as "honorary whites" whose fears can be played against other groups of color regarding affirmative action and admission to elite public universities in California. Yet these groups can also have the law used against them, as it was in the Japanese internment camps during World War II and in current immigration law. CRT has served as an evolving theoretical framework that has been useful when thinking about research, policy, and race. Critical race feminism has also emerged as an area of study with respect to women of color and their connection to the law and public policy's impact on their lives as women, in both the United States and other parts of the world (Wing, 1997). Queer theory, Marxism, and postcolonial theory have also seen connections and conflicts with CRT in terms of historical identity issues and current differing social constructions of race (Delgado and Stefancic, 2000; Valdes, Culp, and Harris, 2002).

CRT has evolved toward the centering of race in the analysis of how it is socially constructed under specific historical and ideological trends and reinforced through legal means. CRT as a research lens can also be used in educational evaluation for analyzing racial inequality in the law and society and how various organizational structures are developing to, in essence, give narrative voice and empowerment to groups that have been traditionally underserved by secondary and postsecondary institutions.

Evaluation in Connection to Critical Race Theory

Evaluation has been traditionally driven by the postpositivist paradigm that places empirical method and rigor over a concern for the population studied. This view of evaluation has often worked against the type of participatory process that has more of a focus on critical social context issues that affect the program and people being studied. Traditional evaluation methods leave much to be desired when the voices of the individuals being studied are excluded from the process.

Given the previous description of CRT, I feel that the field of evaluation needs to fully examine the social context of racism in the broader society; minority groups that are the subjects of the evaluation have to be full participants in the process so evaluators can gain insights from the subjects' perspectives. Conscious subjectivity should be encouraged in the field of evaluation to allow for different points of view in the evaluation process, which can lead to a deeper understanding of the complexity of the issues (Coyner, 1983). Participatory evaluation (Shapiro, 1988) calls for program evaluators to assume the role of independent outsider and knowledgeable insider. Here, the evaluator and the participants can better examine and expose the intended and unintended consequences and benefits of the programs. An evaluator who is a participant in a sense of the member of the group, or has familiarity and trust with that group, is in a better position to ask the right questions to illuminate the complexity of the issue under investigation.

Given the multiple problems related to continued academic racial disparities and administrative policy actions that have a deleterious impact on African American students, the work of the Howard University Center for Research on the Education of Students Placed At Risk (CRESPAR) seeks to provide answers to these problems and to illuminate how collaborative interventions can be used and evaluated in participatory ways for the best interest of African American children and their communities. The Talent Development (TD) model with its six themes holds the staff and students to high standards to educate the whole child, not only with respect to test scores and standardized achievement, but also to enhance the development of the whole child, from character building to social and emotional transformative competencies.

This was the exact intent of the Howard CRESPAR's TD evaluations, particularly regarding how triangulation of perspective is often used to find not one but many answers to a single question. Chapter Two evaluates the co-construction of a school-based family and community partnership for black students in a low-income urban high school. This chapter has crucial implications for policymakers who want to gain insights into what does and does not work regarding these programs, and also how to engage staff and participants in the evaluation process. Chapter Three discusses the successes and challenges related to trying to implement the Talent Development School-to-Career Transitions Intervention program through a culturally responsive evaluation approach. The insights gleaned from this chapter indicate the labor-intensive nature of this type of evaluation, as well as the cultural context of the education setting and the collaborative process among the participants. Chapter Four gives key findings in terms of the importance of co-construction and placing evaluation in the context of the total cultural milieu as critical factors in the evaluation efforts of the Exemplary Schools project. The authors also found that parental involvement was seen as important but not always given primacy by school administrators, a critical finding for future policy concerns about parental involvement in urban schools. Chapter Five calls for the TD evaluation example to serve as a model to look at how to shift the evaluation movement in education to look more comprehensively at the classroom and school and system levels of interaction with regard to student achievement. This chapter also provides a strong outline of key points for readers to take concerning successes and challenges that will affect an evaluation study in the urban context, notably getting the leadership in the schools to realize how the leadership style they set has an impact on the school and professional development activities.

It is here that I think that CRT could be potentially useful as an overall framework for future evaluation studies of this type, given how it has evolved as a methodological perspective on race, the law, and educational policy. Solórzano and Yosso (2002) developed critical race methodology in terms of its utility as an analytical framework to ask research questions, review literature, analyze data, and form conclusions and recommendations. They discussed five tenets of a CRT methodology:

- Placing race and its intersectionality with other forms of subordination at the center of research
- Using race in research to challenge the dominant scientific norms of objectivity and neutrality
- Having the research connected with social justice concerns and potential praxis with ongoing efforts in communities
- Making experiential knowledge central to the study and linking this knowledge to other critical research and interpretive perspectives on race and racism
- Emphasizing the importance of transdisciplinary perspectives that are based in other fields (for example, ethnic studies, women's studies, African American studies, studies on Chicanos and Chicanas and on Latinos and Latinas, history, sociology) for enhancing an understanding of the effects of racism and other forms of discrimination on persons of color

Delgado Bernal (2002) and Tillman (2002) discussed the importance of cultural intuition with respect to using CRT, Chicana feminist epistemology, and African American experiential knowledge for research with Latinas and African Americans. An example of how an evaluation study under CRT and LatCrit can be conceptualized and implemented can be seen in the work of Pizarro (1998). His research in southern California outlined the sociocultural pathways that a group of Latino and Latina students went through regarding their experiences from middle school through college. He wanted to find out when and how race, gender, social class, and language play at particular points in determining life chances for success and failure. He used CRT and LatCrit as his theoretical frameworks, but he also incorporated a participatory evaluation framework in this project in order to fully include the students during every step of the research process. Students were able to talk over the information with Pizarro as a researcher so they could co-interpret the events and discuss how the narratives would be written and for what audience. In some instances, Pizarro also presented the findings with the students at conferences. In this way, a CRT-LatCrit participatory evaluation process was central to the conception and implementation of the study, and the students' voices were indeed heard since they were a part of every step of the research process.

For future evaluation studies of this nature and those developed and implemented by CRESPAR, a CRT methodology and critical race policy analysis for education can be used not only to frame the research issues to study but also to interpret the evidence and provide a lens of focus for racial equity implications. The CRESPAR Talent Development Model of School

Reform is an empowering project for African American education. More on this needs to be heard from the researchers as well as participants in the project. For future evaluations of TD interventions with policy implications, I suggest using the narrative and storytelling aspects of CRT to add more insight and personal reflections from the project participants and evaluators. CRT narratives form powerful counterstories that not only inform readers as to the nature of a project related to educational change, but also speak to inform policy so that policymakers and evaluators in general can learn more about students' families and build and strengthen social networks. The utility of CRT narrative research in education is that the counterstories are an effective tool to challenge myths about the lack of caring and desire that African American and Latino and Latina families have for high-quality education for their children (Auerbach, 2002). Using critical race methodology and critical race policy analysis frameworks for content analysis purposes could provide evaluators with different ways of looking at recurring policy patterns in school leadership and how that has an effect on educational equity for black students.

The future of a critical race theory agenda and its place in educational evaluation of leadership in urban schools for African Americans will partially depend on the efforts made by scholar-activists such as those at Howard University CRESPAR in exploring CRT connections to life in schools and communities of color and to make that testimony a part of the public record and discourse (Yamamoto, 1997). The TD framework described in this volume argues that schools must provide black students with a strong organizational culture or a loving and caring environment for adults and children, with a set of core beliefs that stress that all children can succeed at high academic levels, with the school being learner centered. In conclusion, I think that schools can provide African American students and parents with high student performance goals that can be met through the current climate of accountability if the focus is on changing the culture of schools to meet the educational and emotional needs of the students, parents, and staff to create a community (Scheurich, 1998). The CRESPAR evaluation efforts lead us closer to this and to future studies that will explore the use of CRT to provide answers to the continuing challenge of educating all students to high levels of academic achievement and social competence.

References

Auerbach, S. "'Why Do They Give the Good Classes to Some and Not to Others?' Latino Parent Narratives of Struggle in a College Access Program." *Teachers College Record,* 2002, *104,* 1369–1392.

Chartier, G. "Righting Narrative: Robert Chang, Poststructuralism, and the Possibility of Critique." *UCLA Asian Pacific American Law Journal,* 2001, *7,* 106–132.

Chon, M. "On the Need for Asian American Narratives in Law: Ethnic Specimens, Native Informants, Storytelling and Silences." *UCLA Asian Pacific American Law Journal,* 1995, *3,* 3–32.

Coyner, S. "Women's Studies as an Academic Discipline: Why and How to Do It." In G. Bowles and R. Duelli-Klein (eds.), *Theories in Women's Studies*. London: Routledge, 1983.

Crenshaw, K. W. "The First Decade: Critical Reflections, or 'a Foot in the Closing Door.'" In F. Valdes, J. M. Culp, and A. P. Harris (eds.), *Crossroads, Directions, and a New Critical Race Theory*. Philadelphia: Temple University Press, 2002.

Crenshaw, K. W., Gotanda, N., Peller, G., and Thomas, K. (eds.). *Critical Race Theory: The Key Writings That Formed the Movement*. New York: New Press, 1995.

Delgado, R., and Stefancic, J. *Critical Race Theory: The Cutting Edge.* (2nd ed.) Philadelphia: Temple University Press, 2000.

Delgado Bernal, D. "Critical Race Theory, Latino Critical Theory, and Critical Race-Gendered Epistemologies: Recognizing Students of Color as Holders and Creators of Knowledge." *Qualitative Inquiry,* 2002, *8,* 105–125.

Feagin, J. R. "The Continuing Significance of Racism: Discrimination Against Black Students in White Colleges." *Journal of Black Studies,* 1992, *22,* 546–578.

Goldberg, D. T. *Racist Culture: Philosophy and the Politics of Meaning.* Oxford, U.K.: Blackwell Press, 1993.

Hayman, R. L., Jr. "The Color of Tradition: Critical Race Theory and Postmodern Constitutional Traditionalism." *Harvard Civil Rights-Civil Liberties Law Review,* 1995, *30,* 57–108.

Iglesias, E. "Identity, Democracy, Communicative Power, Inter/National Labor Rights and the Evolution of LatCrit Theory and Community. Special Issue on LatCrit." *University of Miami Law Review,* 1999, *53*(4).

Ladson-Billings, G. "Just What Is Critical Race Theory and What Is It Doing in a Nice Field Like Education?" *International Journal of Qualitative Studies in Education,* 1998, *11,* 7–24.

Lawrence, C. L. III. "Who Are We? And Why Are We Happy? Doing Critical Race Theory in Hard Times." In F. Valdes, J. M. Culp, and A. P. Harris (eds.), *Crossroads, Directions, and a New Critical Race Theory*. Philadelphia: Temple University Press, 2002.

Lopez, G., and Parker, L. (eds.). *Interrogating Racism in Qualitative Research Methodology.* New York: Peter Lang, 2003.

McMorris, G. "Critical Race Theory, Cognitive Psychology, and the Social Meaning of Race: Why Individualism Will Not Solve Racism." *University of Missouri Kansas City Law Review,* 1996, *67,* 695–729.

Parker, L., Deyhle, D., and Villenas, S. (eds.). *Race Is . . . Race Isn't: Critical Race Theory and Qualitative Studies in Education.* Boulder, Colo.: Westview Press, 1999.

Parker, L., and Lynn, M. "What's Race Got to Do with It? Critical Race Theory's Conflicts with and Connections to Qualitative Research Methodology and Epistemology." *Qualitative Inquiry,* 2002, *8,* 7–22.

Pizarro, M. "Chicana/o Power! Epistemology and Methodology for Social Justice and Empowerment in Chicano/a Communities." *International Journal of Qualitative Studies in Education,* 1998, *11,* 57–80.

Scheurich, J. J. "Highly Successful and Loving, Public Elementary Schools Populated Mainly by Low-SES Children of Color: Core Beliefs and Cultural Characteristics." *Urban Education,* 1998, *33,* 451–491.

Shapiro, J. S. "Participatory Evaluation: Towards a Transformative Assessment for Women's Studies Programs and Projects." *Educational Evaluation and Policy Analysis,* 1988, *10,* 191–199.

Solórzano, D. G., and Yosso, T. J. "Critical Race Methodology: Counter-Storytelling as an Analytical Framework for Education Research." *Qualitative Inquiry,* 2002, *8,* 23–44.

Stanfield, J. H. II. "Slipping Through the Front Door: Relevant Social Scientific Evaluation of the People of Color Century." *American Journal of Evaluation,* 1999, *20,* 415–431.

Tate, W. F. IV. "Critical Race Theory and Education: History, Theory, and Implications." In M. Apple (ed.), *Review of Research in Education*. Washington, D.C.: American Educational Research Association, 1997.

Tillman, L. C. "Culturally Sensitive Research Approaches: An African American Perspective." *Educational Researcher*, 2002, *31*, 1–13.

Valdes, F., Culp, J. M., and Harris, A. P. *Crossroads, Directions, and a New Critical Race Theory*. Philadelphia: Temple University Press, 2002.

Wing, A. K. (ed.). *Critical Race Feminism*. New York: New York University Press, 1997.

Yamamoto, E. "Critical Race Praxis: Race Theory and Political Lawyering in Post–Civil Rights America." *Michigan Law Review*, 1997, *95*, 821–900.

LAURENCE PARKER is associate professor in the Department of Educational Policy Studies at the University of Illinois at Urbana-Champaign.

INDEX

Abma, T. A., 7, 13, 38
Accelerated Schools, 4
Adger, C., 76
Administrators: benefits of co-construction to, 10; effect of, on professional development evaluation, 75; forms of, 50; priorities of, 16
Affirmative action, 87–88
African American evaluators, 12
African American students, 90–91
Alexander, W., 5
American Evaluation Association, 17, 18
Analysis triangulation, 14
Analyzing data, 44
Argyris, C., 27
Arrendondo, P., 11
Asset-based approach, 34
Attendance log, 31
Auerbach, S., 91
Ayres, R., 38, 74

Bain, R., 63
Behavior standards, 56
Ben-Avie, M., 4
Berger, E. H., 25, 26
Berry, J. W., 11
Boykin, A. W., 4, 5, 11, 25, 26, 34, 49, 50, 64
Brandon, P. R., 27, 30, 38
Breakfast Club, 40–46
Brotherton, P., 25
Budgets, 58
Building, school, 54
Business-casual attire, 32, 33

Campbell, D. T., 14
Caracelli, V. J., 14, 43, 51, 74
Carey, R. G., 26
Carroll, G., 9, 10, 11, 15, 26, 50
Cassaro, D. A., 38
Casual business attire, 32, 33
Center for Research on the Education of Students Placed At Risk (CRESPAR), 1, 2; challenges of, 15–17; co-construction in, 9–10; culture and context in, 10–13; in development of partnership programs, 26; influences on, 7; overview of, 4–5, 39–40; purposes of, 6, 89; respon-

siveness in, 13–14; schools served by, 5; stakeholder involvement in, 7–8; themes of, 7; triangulation in, 14–15; use of results from, 5–6
Chartier, G., 87
Chelimsky, E., 8
Chon, M., 87
Clair, N., 76
Climate, school, 55–56
Coalition of Essential Schools, 4
Co-construction: benefits of, 10; in culturally responsive evaluation process, 42; overview of, 9–10, 81; versus participatory approaches, 9–10; recommendations for, 18; in Talent Development Professional Development process, 71–72
Coherence, 80–83
Cole, K. C., 11
Cole-Henderson, B., 51
Comer, J., 4, 57
Community activities, 13
Community partnership programs. *See* Partnership programs
Conflicting priorities, 16
Content, definition of, 69
Context: and asset-based approach, 34; definition of, 11, 38, 69; importance of, 66; overview of, 81; in Talent Development Professional Development process, 70–71
Cousins, J. B., 7, 9, 27, 38, 67
Coyner, S., 88
Crenshaw, K. W., 85
CRESPAR. *See* Center for Research on the Education of Students Placed At Risk (CRESPAR)
Critical race theory (CRT): and evaluation, 88–91; overview of, 85–88
Cuban, L., 49
Culp, J. M., 88
Cultural competence: definition of, 11; need for, 66
Culturally responsive evaluations: challenges of, 45–46; definition of, 59; drawbacks of, 39; implications of, 45; overview of, 38–39; phases of, 41; of School-to-Career Transitions intervention, 41–46; and triangulation, 59–60

Back Issue/Subscription Order Form

Copy or detach and send to:
Jossey-Bass, A Wiley Imprint, 989 Market Street, San Francisco CA 94103-1741

Call or fax toll-free: Phone 888-378-2537 6:30AM – 3PM PST; Fax 888-481-2665

Back Issues: Please send me the following issues at $27 each
(Important: please include series abbreviation and issue number.
For example EV93)

_____

_____

_____

$ _____   Total for single issues

$ _____   SHIPPING CHARGES: SURFACE   Domestic Canadian
First Item $5.00 $6.00
Each Add'l Item $3.00 $1.50
For next-day and second-day delivery rates, call the number listed above.

Subscriptions   Please __start __renew my subscription to *New Directions for Evaluation* for the year 2____at the following rate:

U.S.	__Individual $80	__Institutional $175
Canada	__Individual $80	__Institutional $215
All Others	__Individual $104	__Institutional $249
Online Subscription		__Institutional $193

**For more information about online subscriptions visit
www.interscience.wiley.com**

$ _____   Total single issues and subscriptions (Add appropriate sales tax for your state for single issue orders. No sales tax for U.S. subscriptions. Canadian residents, add GST for subscriptions and single issues.)

__Payment enclosed (U.S. check or money order only)
__VISA __MC __ AmEx # _____ Exp. Date _____

Signature _____ Day Phone _____
__ Bill Me (U.S. institutional orders only. Purchase order required.)

Purchase order # _____
Federal Tax ID13559302   GST 89102 8052

Name _____

Address _____

_____

Phone _____ E-mail _____

For more information about Jossey-Bass, visit our Web site at www.josseybass.com

NEW DIRECTIONS FOR EVALUATION
IS NOW AVAILABLE ONLINE AT WILEY INTERSCIENCE

What is Wiley InterScience?

Wiley InterScience is the dynamic online content service from John Wiley & Sons delivering the full text of over 300 leading scientific, technical, medical, and professional journals, plus major reference works, the acclaimed Current Protocols laboratory manuals, and even the full text of select Wiley print books online.

What are some special features of Wiley InterScience?

Wiley Interscience Alerts is a service that delivers table of contents via e-mail for any journal available on Wiley InterScience as soon as a new issue is published online.
Early View is Wiley's exclusive service presenting individual articles online as soon as they are ready, even before the release of the compiled print issue. These articles are complete, peer-reviewed, and citable.
CrossRef is the innovative multi-publisher reference linking system enabling readers to move seamlessly from a reference in a journal article to the cited publication, typically located on a different server and published by a different publisher.

How can I access Wiley InterScience?

Visit http://www.interscience.wiley.com.

Guest Users can browse Wiley InterScience for unrestricted access to journal Tables of Contents and Article Abstracts, or use the powerful search engine.
Registered Users are provided with a *Personal Home Page* to store and manage customized alerts, searches, and links to favorite journals and articles. Additionally, Registered Users can view free Online Sample Issues and preview selected material from major reference works.
Licensed Customers are entitled to access full-text journal articles in PDF, with select journals also offering full-text HTML.

How do I become an Authorized User?

Authorized Users are individuals authorized by a paying Customer to have access to the journals in Wiley InterScience. For example, a University that subscribes to Wiley journals is considered to be the Customer. Faculty, staff and students authorized by the University to have access to those journals in Wiley InterScience are Authorized Users. Users should contact their Library for information on which Wiley journals they have access to in Wiley InterScience.

4990 51

ASK YOUR INSTITUTION ABOUT WILEY INTERSCIENCE TODAY!